SON of a SOUTHERN CHEF

#MAKEITGRAVY

SON of a SOUTHERN CHEF
COOK WITH SOUL

LAZARUS LYNCH

Photography by
ANISHA SISODIA

AVERY

AN IMPRINT OF PENGUIN RANDOM HOUSE | NEW YORK

THE PEOPLE'S

ROCKSTAR CHEF

WHO LIVES BOLD AND

COOKS WITH SOUL.

𝒜
AVERY

an imprint of Penguin Random House LLC
penguinrandomhouse.com

Most Avery books are available at special quantity discounts for bulk purchase
for sales promotions, premiums, fund-raising, and educational needs. Special
books or book excerpts also can be created to fit specific needs. For details,
write SpecialMarkets@penguinrandomhouse.com.

Library of Congress Cataloging-in-Publication Data
Names: Lynch, Lazarus, author.
Title: Son of a Southern chef : cook with soul / Lazarus Lynch.
Description: New York : Avery, an imprint of Penguin Random House, [2019] |
Includes index.
Identifiers: LCCN 2018059322| ISBN 9780525534174 (trade pbk.) |
ISBN 9780525534181 (ebook)
Subjects: LCSH: Cooking, American--Southern style. |
LCGFT: Cookbooks.
Classification: LCC TX715.2.S68 L96 2019 |
DDC 641.5975--dc23 LC record available at
https://lccn.loc.gov/2018059322
p.   cm.

Printed in China
10 9 8 7 6 5 4 3 2 1

Book design by Ashley Tucker

METERED
FARE

This book is humbly dedicated to my
late father, Johnny Ray Lynch, and to my
loving mother, Debbie-Ann, for giving
me a lifetime of unconditional love and
inspiring me to live my dreams! I love you
and hope to always make you proud!

Your son, Lazarus

CONTENTS

INTRODUCTION

Spoiler alert: I'm not from the South! I was born and bred in Southside Jamaica, Queens, the part of New York City where rappers like Nas, 50 Cent, and LL Cool J got their start. I come from the hustle and the bustle, the big city lights in Times Square, where you share subway rides to high school with regular folks and celebrities, who are just regular folks. I come from art classes on weekends; church dinners with church friends; and generations of strong men and women who helped raise me, instilled self-respect, and made sure I kept my manners. Yes, sir, yes, ma'am, that's a fact.

My love affair with food started long before being a "foodie" on Instagram was a thing; it started with Dad: the Southern chef.

As a kid, I remember watching my dad roll out his butter or lard-filled pastry dough in our kitchen for his famous peach cobbler. The smell of hot peaches soaking in cinnamon and sugar, combined with that flaky, buttery crust, filled the house with an everlasting aroma. Dad loved to cook; he loved feeding us—Mom, my three siblings, and me.

We could not wait for the days when Dad would bring home big white buckets filled with live crab from the fish market on Jamaica Avenue. Like the champ he was, he would toss the crabs into our kitchen sink with his bare hands, give them a good ol' washing, then transfer them into a large pot of seasoned hot water and cook them to perfection. Then he would unwrap a pound of butter, literally the size of a brick, melt it in a hot cast-iron skillet, season it with Old Bay and garlic powder, then serve the crab legs on large plates with lemon wedges, and a loving pour of the melted butter, family-style. This kind of cooking wasn't unusual in our household. This is how we got down. Cooking with Dad was my definition of home.

My childhood food world consisted of big, shared Sunday lunches after church, bacon-egg-and-cheese sandwiches from the bodega, and 12 a.m. impromptu cook-ups with Dad. My neighborhood was a melting pot of cultures and cuisines that came together to form one community. I was always fascinated by the pockets of Jackson Heights that had some of the most amazing samosas and curries, and Hillside Avenue for its authentic Guyanese and Trinidadian pastries. I people-watched as the elders of my community congregated, telling the stories of yesterday and playing cards while grooving to Marvin Gaye. I was surrounded by the glories of good people and good food, food that had meaning and soul.

My father, Johnny Ray Lynch, grew up in the small town of Bessemer, Alabama—the Marvel City. He started cooking when he was thirteen, at the hip of his late mother, Margarette Louise Lynch, and late grandmother Louise Sledge. They were housekeepers, beauticians, and phenomenal cooks who showed him the way to real country cooking. Everything my father knew about cooking, he learned from them, and not once did he rely on a cookbook.

My folks approached cooking from a gut level. Cooking was all about pure instinct, being resourceful, and being thankful.

People ask me all the time why I became a chef, and I wish I had a deep answer. The short answer is that I really love food, every aspect of it. I went to Food and Finance High School in Manhattan's Hell's Kitchen to refine my cooking sensibilities, but the truth is that cooking is in my blood.

I was ten years old when my parents opened a restaurant, Baby Sister's Soul Food, in Queens. It was their first attempt at running a restaurant in a predominantly black community, and a chance for my father to revive the slowly dying soul food cuisine in our 'hood. My father had no real idea what to expect, how long the restaurant would survive, or who would eat there. It was all-or-nothing, and those were the principles he lived by. The first location stood adjacent to a convenience store on Farmers Boulevard in St. Albans, Queens. Eventually, the rent got too damn high and my parents relocated the restaurant to Laurelton, Queens, where Dad's was one of at least a dozen restaurants in less than a one-mile radius.

My mother, Debbie-Ann, was a full-time secretary by day and sous chef by night. Let me back up. Mom grew up in Georgetown, Guyana, then moved to London, England, when she was thirteen. By her mid-twenties, she was moonlighting at clubs and restaurants, serving the British posh. She moved to New York City back in the eighties, hopped around from Long Island to Brooklyn, then back to Long Island, then finally to Queens, where she and my dad were neighbors. They fell in love,

and the rest was, as they say, history.

Anyway, every day, Mom faithfully left her nine-to-five to put in another five-hour shift at the restaurant with Dad. Dropping orders of fried fish and chips and greeting piles of dirty dishes were just some of her duties. Mom loved Dad, and every part of the business—except for the cooking, ironically. Mom is a decent cook, but doesn't really enjoy it. She can make a mean pot of saltfish with boiled dumplings, green banana, Japanese sweet potatoes, and fried sweet plantain. As a kid, Mom cooked a new meal every night for six people, including herself, and more if we were randomly entertaining guests. She helped us with homework, washed our dishes, cleaned the house, put us to bed, and still had time to travel the world, read 500-plus-page novels, and serve as a missionary at our church. Mom was Dad's number-one fan and stood behind him through thick and thin. They were a team. They were lovers. And they were friends.

The restaurant had a very basic menu: fried fish, fried shrimp, fried okra, fried broccoli, French fries (I know, so much fried stuff), coleslaw, potato salad, and macaroni salad. Each fish dinner was served with a choice of wheat or white bread and Dad's classic tartar sauce. There were other items on the menu, too, like macaroni and cheese, black-eyed peas, candied yams, collard greens, and my brother's banana pudding, but these were seldom available. It all depended on the day, Dad's mood, or the mood of the cash register.

Dad was an all-around artist. He played the saxophone and bass guitar, and loved to sing along to oldies like Barry White on the stage he built at the restaurant on slow days. My father installed carpet for years before opening the restaurant. He named that store Lazarus Carpet, after me. Prior to that, he owned a men's retail clothing store, then a 99-cent variety store. And prior to all that, he owned a moving service business. He traded it all for the calling to be a chef, a life filled with unimaginable uncertainty and adventure.

My father's dream restaurant was one that would serve the best soul food in New York City and feature live musical performances every night. In 2014, he was approached by a big television network that wanted to feature his famous macaroni and cheese in a new food and travel show. Dad was too ill at the time to proceed with the production, though he tried convincing the producers he would be well for the shoot. He was in his early stages of cancer and was in complete denial about his condition.

My father defined hard work better than anybody. He had a deep need to be successful and an even greater need not to fail. He had an addiction to work—an addiction I resented as a kid. He started his days around noon and finished around midnight. He took no vacations, worked on holidays and weekends, and rarely had a sick day. Dad never knew his father. He thought being a dad meant providing a roof over our heads and putting food in our bellies. And that's just what he did. How could a man know how to do something he has never been shown before? He just wanted to be a good father. I found myself longing for my father, and bonding with him in the kitchen became our way of life.

THE MAKING OF SON OF A SOUTHERN CHEF

I created Son of a Southern Chef in 2014. At the time, I was a sophomore at SUNY Buffalo State College, going through the motions of higher education in a major I no longer loved. I had a desperate need to focus my energy on something I truly cared about, something that spoke to my soul. That year, I thought a lot about everything: Dad and our family, my love for cooking, how I got started, the way my father built his career from scratch much like the way his mother made cakes. All this searching led me to discover the untold story of my roots, who I was, and what I wanted to be. I spent hours interviewing my father and his relatives and gathering recipes. I made audio and visual recordings of him, learning as much as I could about his life, his dreams, and the food of our family. I documented the recipes that were passed down through two generations, to him and now to me. I saw the deeper connection my father and I had through the food we made together. I knew my generation needed to learn from the previous one and that we also had something to teach.

I eventually recruited friends on campus to help me shoot a cooking show in my dorm that I called *My College Kitchen*, and promised them the best food they would ever find on campus in return for their services, LOL. It worked! I started posting these videos on YouTube and was introduced to the world as Son of a Southern Chef.

I quickly began to see the power of social media as my Instagram exploded. People near

and far DM'd me asking me to cater events and private parties or teach them how to make *real* mac and cheese and collard greens. By September 2015, I was discovered by Tastemade Network, and shortly after, I started making videos with them for Snapchat in Los Angeles, California. Months later, ABC Network casted me in an original digital show, *Tastemade Get Cooking*. All the while, I was still a full-time college student, writing papers in airports and grinding out my YouTube videos with my friends on the weekends. I was living my dream, hustling my way to the top, just as I'd learned from Dad.

On January 9, 2015, just months before things started to take off, my mother received a devastating phone call that my father had passed away. The cancer had metastasized, spreading from his prostate to his bones, and eventually, to his brain, and he had been hospitalized that New Year's Day. I came to a complete standstill emotionally. I second-guessed the future of Son of a Southern Chef. I had just found the work I was passionate about in connection with my father, but it felt like it was being pulled from under my feet. Then I was reminded of something my father had said to me in an interview the year before: "Lazarus should take what I'm doing in another direction and into another level . . ."

My father's death, which I now refer to as his "transition," was one of the toughest experiences I've been through. But it also taught me so many beautiful lessons. It showed me how to pursue joy in the midst of tragedy, how to trust, believe, and act on my dreams, and how to deepen my trust and faith in God. I realized the gift of cooking my father gave to me was not only for me, but it was something to be shared with the world.

I don't think my father ever dreamed of becoming a chef, nor did he even consider himself to be one after he opened Baby Sister's. What I know to be true is this: My father passed down a lifetime of delectable recipes, full of soul, inherited from generations of Southern women and men who loved making good food. I am so grateful to honor his legacy in a global way and reach an entirely new generation with soul food. I don't claim to know everything about soul food—I'm still learning. Son of a Southern Chef is the beginning of the work I believe I am here to do. My father never strived to be perfect in the kitchen, only to make good food, and that's my goal for every reader of this book.

MAKE IT GRAVY!
BLESSINGS AND BACON GREASE,

Lazarus

THE ROCKSTAR KITCHEN

The right kitchen swag gives me rockstar vibes. By that I mean, when I have the basics on lock, the possibilities of what I can create are enormous. Every cook and kitchen is different, but having the fundamentals down makes you a freakin' rockstar in the kitchen! Leggo.

KOSHER SALT

I use Morton's kosher salt in my kitchen and for most of these recipes. It's an easy salt to pick up and sprinkle like @Nuser_et#Saltbae (okay, but why is he so famous tho, lmbo . . . goals). Diamond brand is good, too, though teaspoon for teaspoon it is less salty than Morton. If you use Diamond salt, you may need a pinch more to season. All the recipes provide my suggested amounts of salt and pepper, though you should taste and adjust seasonings to your personal preferences, mmkay.

FLAKY OR FINE SEA SALT

I love to use a fat pinch of flaky sea salt when finishing dishes like fried chicken or as a topping on chocolate ice cream. I like using fine sea salt when I'm baking because of its pure salt flavor. I prefer any type of coarse salt like flaky Maldon or Morton's sea salt. Please don't use table salt! It's treated with iodine, which tastes metallic when cooked, and I'm just not a fan of it.

FRESHLY GROUND BLACK PEPPER

You will notice that all my recipes that use black pepper call for "*freshly* ground black pepper" because that pre-ground stuff at the grocery store has lost all its kick. The fresher the grind, the better the taste.

JAMAICAN-STYLE YELLOW CURRY POWDER

I say later in the book that we "curry" everything in my household, and it's so true. There are as many types of curry powders in the world as there are weirdos. We must live with this reality, people. Whenever I call for curry powder, I am specifically calling for Jamaican-style yellow curry powder. I've tried so many different brands over the years and still have no favorites (sorry). If you cannot find Jamaican-style, use a sweet curry powder instead; it's a great rich and balanced substitute. If curry stains your pots, fill the pot with cold water and boil the water until the curry releases from the pot and the water turns yellow. Wash the pot with hot soapy water.

HOT SAUCE

Bring on the heat, baby! In my household, we usually have at least five different kinds of hot sauces ranging from Caribbean hot pepper sauce to Sriracha. In the recipes where I call for "hot sauce," use whatever brand of vinegar-based hot sauce you love the most, unless otherwise specified.

BROWNING SAUCE

Some of my Caribbean-inspired dishes call for browning sauce, which is a dark sauce made of cane sugar, caramel, and salt—not to be confused with Worcestershire sauce, made from vinegar, anchovies, molasses, and tamarind. Browning sauce is really good for adding dark color to stews, sauces, and meats. I use Grace brand, which is just labeled as "Browning." Kitchen Bouquet is an acceptable substitute (if you must).

SCOTCH BONNET PEPPER

The Scotch bonnet pepper is widely used in Jamaican and Caribbean cooking, and I love it for its blast of heat. Trust me, a little goes a long way. If you can't find Scotch bonnet peppers, use habaneros. If you can't find habaneros, use jalapeños. If you can't find jalapeños, you should probably move (just kidding)! As with all hot peppers, don't touch your eyes or sensitive areas after handling. Wash your hands thoroughly after touching the peppers, or just wear gloves as an extra precaution.

MAPLE SYRUP

I use maple syrup a lot, like it's going out of style, but it ain't cheap. There are two main types of maple. Grade A, which is lighter in color, and grade B, which is darker in color. Honestly, they're all the same to me. I don't care which one you use, unless one is on sale, in which case, choose what's best for your wallet.

BUTTER

Butter is one of those things I'm very particular about. First of all, it must be *real*—made from cream—never margarine. The reason I use unsalted butter in baking is because each brand of salted butter has a different amount of salt in it, which will result in flavor inconsistencies on your end. However, I LOVE salted butter on my toast or on top of sweet potatoes!

UNBLEACHED ALL-PURPOSE FLOUR

I go for unbleached all-purpose flour, because I feel it is purer.

EGGS

As a standard, I use large eggs, unless otherwise specified in the recipe. Using a different size egg than the one called for can change the entire liquid ratio in a recipe, so stick with large and all will go well for you.

MEASURING INGREDIENTS

When I was a high school intern at the Food Network, they taught me the right way to measure ingredients. For dry ingredients (flour, cornmeal, rice, etc.), use dry measuring cups, the kind that (usually) look like scoops and come in ¼-, ⅓-, ½-, and 1-cup sizes. For accuracy, use a spoon to scoop the dry ingredient into the measuring cup and level off the top with the back of a knife. Don't tap the cup on the counter or you'll knock air out and compress the ingredient, which can affect the measurement and, in cases like baked goods where exact measures are important, the end result. For wet ingredients (milk, buttermilk, etc.), use a liquid measuring cup, the kind that (usually) has a spout for pouring—Pyrex is a common brand.

Sometimes the same quantity of an ingredient can be expressed in two (or more—hey, butter!) different ways. This can be helpful if you're dividing the ingredient to use at different points in a recipe. Here are some basic equivalents for you:

Measurement Equivalents

- ♥ 3 teaspoons = 1 tablespoon
- ♥ 4 tablespoons = ¼ cup
- ♥ 2 tablespoons = 1 fluid ounce
- ♥ 1 cup = 8 fluid ounces
- ♥ 2 cups = 1 pint
- ♥ 1 stick butter = 8 tablespoons or ½ cup or 4 ounces or ¼ pound
- ♥ 1 large onion, chopped = about 2 cups
- ♥ 1 medium onion, chopped = about 1 cup
- ♥ 2 garlic cloves, minced = about 1 tablespoon

TOASTING NUTS

I toast a lot of nuts in this book. Rather than giving you instructions in every recipe, here's all you need to know about toasting nuts:

Oven Method

Preheat the oven to 350°F. Spread the nuts over a rimmed baking sheet and toast in the oven for 7 to 10 minutes, shaking the pan occasionally and checking to make sure the nuts aren't burning. Use your nose.

Skillet Method

In a dry skillet (meaning no oil or water in it), toast the nuts over medium heat, shaking the pan or stirring occasionally, until the nuts are warmed and smell . . . well, nutty, 2 to 3 minutes.

EQUIPMENT

- ♥ **Wooden spoon**
- ♥ **Flexible rubber spatula**
  (for scrambling eggs)
- ♥ **Metal spatula**
  (for flipping stuff)
- ♥ **Metal whisk**
- ♥ **Tongs**
- ♥ **Strainer**
- ♥ **Pepper grinder**
- ♥ **Vegetable peeler**
- ♥ **Large pot**
  (for boiling water and frying)
- ♥ **Large sauté pan**
- ♥ **Potato masher**
- ♥ **Dry measuring cups**
  (for dry ingredients like flour)
- ♥ **Liquid measuring cups**
  (for wet ingredients like milk)
- ♥ **Measuring spoons**
- ♥ **Microplane grater**
- ♥ **Candy thermometer**
  (for deep-frying)
- ♥ **Digital thermometer**
  (for birds and meats)
- ♥ **Oven thermometer**
  (to make sure your oven isn't spazzing)
- ♥ **Cooling rack**

BONUS EQUIPMENT

- ♥ **Salad spinner**
- ♥ **Food processor**
- ♥ **Blender**
- ♥ **Immersion blender**
- ♥ **Stand mixer**
- ♥ **Blow torch**
- ♥ **Electric hand mixer**

MORE ON NUTS . . .

If you happen to live with someone with nut allergies, use a separate cutting board or piece of parchment paper to chop nuts. Some of the recipes in this book that call for nuts can be made without them, in which case I've labeled them "(optional)." In addition, if a recipe calls for peanut oil, canola or vegetable oil are good substitutes.

A GOOD CHEF'S KNIFE

I emphasize *good*. Knives come in all shapes and sizes, and some cost more than others. In general, knives are an investment. A good-quality chef's knife will cut through anything with very little effort. You want a chef's knife that you feel comfortable holding in your hand; comfort is key. I like having a chef's knife, boning knife (for trimming meats, poultry, or fish), paring knife (for peeling and trimming small fruits and vegetables), and a serrated knife (aka a bread knife). Keep your knives protected by storing them on a magnetic knife stip (instead of a knife block), and keep them sharp with a benchstone and butcher steels.(Consult with Google for more info.)

CAST-IRON SKILLET

If you don't have one, put down this book right now and go buy one; they're super-affordable! Always clean your cast-iron skillet with warm water, no soap, and use coarse salt to scrub off any grit. Dry the skillet on the stove and rub with a thin layer of canola or vegetable oil. I recommend a 10- or 12-inch cast-iron skillet, which is like $22 USD and lasts forever!

In General . . .

SAFETY FIRST

Put a damp cloth underneath your cutting board to keep it from sliding when you're slicing and dicing.

CROSS CONTAMINATION

Use separate cutting boards for meats and vegetables. Rinse all fresh produce, herbs, and protein before using (rinsing with cold water and lemon is good).

REUSE YOUR WASTE

Don't throw away your onion, garlic, and carrot peels. Keep them, along with leftover bones, and use them to make stock. Waste not, want not.

TASTE EVERYTHING

Not only will your taste buds appreciate it, but so will others you're serving. You can always under-season and add more salt, but taking out salt is much harder.

KNIFE CUTS

- ♥ **Rough chop** means whatever you want. They can be irregular in size.
- ♥ **Large dice** means 1 inch by 1 inch by 1 inch.
- ♥ **Medium dice** means ½ inch by ½ inch by ½ inch.
- ♥ **Small dice** means ¼ inch by ¼ inch by ¼ inch.
- ♥ **Mince means** fine pieces. Hold down the front of your knife on the cutting board with your hand and move the knife up and down over the ingredient.
- ♥ **Fine mince** means super-fine pieces. Lay the knife perpendicular to the cutting board and drag the sharp part of the knife over the ingredient several times to turn it into a paste.
- ♥ **Julienne** is a cute name and means cutting into matchsticks.
- ♥ **Chiffonade** means thin strips. Roll the ingredient up like a cigar and rock out thin strips.

PREP TIME

This is the total amount of time it takes to measure, chop, and weigh ingredients before you begin the action of cooking. Most cooking times are rounded up, and they are the average time it took me to measure, chop, and weigh everything before I started cooking.

TOTAL TIME

This time includes prep time, active and inactive cooking times, and cooling times. Like the prep times, this time is averaged up to the nearest 5 minutes. For some recipes that give a big range of times (for example, marinate meat for 30 minutes up to 2 hours), the total time will reflect the *least* amount of time suggested, e.g., 30 minutes. For baking recipes, I round up to the nearest hour.

THE GRAVY

These are my tips! You know, like "the scoop"? The secrets to all my recipes and being a rockstar kitchen genius are in "the gravy."

KEEP IT SIMPLE: LIVE BOLD AND COOK WITH SOUL. MAKE IT GRAVY!

—*Lazarus Lynch*

STAY WOKE

DAD'S SALMON CROQUETTES WITH OVER-EASY EGGS <u>AND</u> AVOCADO DRESSING

SERVES 6 **PREP TIME** 10 MINUTES **TOTAL TIME** 25 MINUTES

DRESSING

1 ripe Hass avocado, pitted and peeled

¼ cup mayonnaise

2 tablespoons red wine vinegar or fresh lemon juice

1 tablespoon finely chopped fresh cilantro leaves

Few dashes of your favorite hot sauce, plus more to taste

Kosher salt and freshly ground black pepper

SALMON CROQUETTES

7 large eggs

1 (14.75-ounce) can Alaskan pink salmon, bones and skin removed

½ cup minced red or green bell peppers, or a mix

½ cup plain breadcrumbs

2 scallions, finely chopped (about 2 tablespoons)

3 teaspoons garlic powder

Kosher salt and freshly ground black pepper

¼ cup all-purpose flour

¼ cup cornmeal

We ate a lot of canned foods growing up (and we thought EVERY-ONE did, so . . . be nice). My dad's infamous salmon croquettes used canned salmon that he jazzed up. Literally, the croquettes were the size of his hands (which translates to the average size of a human face). They were deep-fried until golden brown and served on sliced bread with tartar sauce—they were so damn good! I figured, *How do I transform this recipe into a happy brunch for a bunch of Brooklyn hipsters?* Easy—keep the canned salmon, and add some avocado and a runny egg on top! Yup. It's everything you want for brunch without the hassle of waiting in a crazy-long line or spending your rent money. This classic just went from ninety-nine to a hundred, real quick.

Make the dressing: In a blender or food processor, combine the avocado, mayo, vinegar, cilantro, hot sauce, and 2 tablespoons water and blend until smooth. Season with salt, pepper, and additional hot sauce as desired.

Make the croquettes: In a small bowl, beat 1 egg with a fork.

In a large bowl, use a spoon to mix together the beaten egg, salmon, bell peppers, breadcrumbs, scallions, 1½ teaspoons of the garlic powder, ½ teaspoon salt, and ¼ teaspoon black pepper. Form the mixture into six ¼-cup-size patties and set aside.

In a shallow baking dish or bowl, use a fork to mix together the flour, cornmeal, remaining 1½ teaspoons garlic powder, ½ teaspoon salt, and ¼ teaspoon black pepper. Dredge the croquette patties in the flour mixture.

RECIPE AND INGREDIENTS CONTINUE ⟫

Vegetable oil, for frying

3 cups baby watercress or other peppery greens, such as arugula

Cracked black pepper, for garnish

In a large cast-iron skillet, heat ¼ cup oil over medium-high heat until it shimmers, about 3 minutes. Gently lay the croquettes in the skillet and fry until golden brown on one side, 2 to 3 minutes. Using a metal spatula, flip each croquette and fry until golden brown on the other side, 2 to 3 minutes more. Add 1 tablespoon more oil if the pan looks dry. Transfer the croquettes to a paper towel–lined plate to drain and cover lightly with aluminum foil to keep warm.

In a large nonstick skillet, heat 2 tablespoons oil over medium heat for about 1 minute. Crack 3 eggs, one at a time, into a small bowl (to prevent shells from getting into the cooked eggs) and gently pour each egg into a section of the skillet. Cook the eggs until the whites are set and the yolks are just beginning to set, about 3 minutes. Gently flip the eggs, one at a time, and cook for 15 seconds more. Remove the eggs from the pan and repeat with the remaining 3 eggs.

Divide the watercress evenly among six plates and top each plate with a croquette, followed by an egg, some avocado dressing, salt, and cracked pepper. Serve A$AP ROCKY.

GUYANESE BAKE

SERVES 10 **PREP TIME** 40 MINUTES **TOTAL TIME** 1 HOUR

3 cups all-purpose flour

1 tablespoon baking powder

2 teaspoons sugar

¼ teaspoon fine salt

1 tablespoon unsalted butter,
  at room temperature

Canola or vegetable oil,
  for frying

Mom's Saltfish (page 30)
  or stuffing of your choice

Fried "bake" or "float" are to the Guyanese what bagels are to the Jews. Everything belongs inside the bake, like a pouch, and it is a typical breakfast food. I like to stuff my bake with Mom's Saltfish, or go American and make scrambled eggs. Either way, the bake is clutch for pocketing any food you wish.

In a large bowl, mix together the flour, baking powder, sugar, and salt. With your fingers, thoroughly work all the butter into the flour mixture. Add 1 cup room-temperature water and mix with your hands to form a smooth and soft dough. Be careful not to overmix, or your dough will be tough! Add up to ¼ cup additional water if the mixture feels too dry. Cover the bowl with a damp cloth and let the dough rest for at least 30 minutes.

Fill a large pot with oil to a depth of 3 inches and heat the oil over medium-high heat to 350°F.

On a lightly floured surface, knead the dough for 1 minute. Divide the dough into 10 equal pieces and roll out each piece into a 4-inch round.

Working with one round at a time, drop the dough into the hot oil—it will sink to the bottom, then float to the top within seconds. Using a long metal spoon, continuously spoon the hot oil over the top of the dough as it starts to puff up, 1 to 2 minutes. As soon as the dough puffs up and turns golden brown on one side, flip it and cook until golden brown on the other side, about 2 minutes more. Using a slotted spoon, transfer the bakes to a paper towel–lined plate to drain. Repeat with the remaining dough.

To serve, insert a knife into the bake to make a pocket and stuff with ¼ cup saltfish or stuffing of your choice.

MOM'S SALTFISH

SERVES 10 TO 12   **PREP TIME** 10 MINUTES   **TOTAL TIME** 2 HOURS

Two (12-ounce) packages dried boneless salted cod or pollock

3 tablespoons canola oil

1 large yellow onion

1 large vine-ripe or beefsteak tomato, chopped

1 bunch scallions, thinly sliced

2 garlic cloves, finely chopped

¼ teaspoon freshly ground black pepper

Lemon wedges, for serving

Guyanese Bakes (page 29), for serving

Rice, for serving

Red Hot Pepper Sauce (page 204), for serving

I am always surprised how much people love my mom's saltfish when they taste it for the first time; even the pickiest eaters LOVE saltfish. Saltfish is salted cod that is dried and preserved. It's really salty, so you need to boil it in fresh water for a while or soak it overnight to remove the salt and tenderize the fish. This might be the one recipe everyone in my household knows how to make, since my mom has been making saltfish all our lives. I love eating this over white rice or with Guyanese Bake (page 29) and boiled Japanese sweet potatoes and sweet plantains. Thanks, Mom—you've really outdone yourself here.

Bring a large pot of water to a rapid bowl. Add the cod and boil for about 1 hour. Drain the cod in a colander. Fill the pot with fresh cold water and bring it to a boil. Return the cod to the pot and boil for 30 minutes more. Drain the cod and fluff it with two forks. Set aside.

Heat the oil in a Dutch oven or heavy-bottomed pot over medium-high heat. Add the onion, tomato, scallions, and garlic and cook, stirring occasionally, until tender, about 8 minutes. Add the cod and black pepper and reduce the heat to low. Cook to let the flavors meld, stirring occasionally, for about 15 minutes. Squeeze a lemon wedge over the fish before serving.

Serve the codfish with my Guyanese Bakes, rice, and hot sauce.

GUYANESE BAKE
(page 29)

MOM'S SALTFISH
(page 30)

THE GRAVY

The grits will thicken as they sit. Use more stock or milk to loosen them up.

SHRIMP AND CRAZY CREAMY CHEDDAR GRITS

SERVES 4 **PREP TIME** 15 MINUTES **TOTAL TIME** 45 MINUTES

GRITS

1¾ cups chicken stock, plus more as needed

One (13.5-ounce can) unsweetened full-fat coconut milk

1 cup whole milk or heavy cream, plus more as needed

1 cup stone-ground white grits

Kosher salt and freshly ground black pepper

4 ounces extra-sharp white cheddar cheese, grated

3 tablespoons unsalted butter

SHRIMP

2 tablespoons extra-virgin olive oil

2 garlic cloves, minced

¼ cup dry white wine

1 pound jumbo shrimp, peeled and deveined

½ teaspoon kosher salt

½ teaspoon freshly ground black pepper

¼ cup chicken stock

1 tablespoon unsalted butter, chilled

2 teaspoons fresh lemon juice

Dash of hot sauce

Pinch of cayenne pepper

1 tablespoon chopped parsley

Honestly, it's shrimp and grits. It's classic. It's luxurious. It screams "yasssss." . . . Need I say more? And I was that kid who ONLY ate grits with sugar and butter. I couldn't wrap my six-year-old brain around why anyone would add salt and pepper to their grits. As I grew up, I began to appreciate the savory version, though I was never completely sold—until now. And that, my friends, has delivered to you the magic that is this recipe. These grits are smooth and creamy, and yes, baby, they're hella rich. I promise you've never had shrimp and grits like these before, and you'll never, ever want to eat normal shrimp and grits again. Watch.

Make the grits: Bring the chicken stock, coconut milk, and milk to a boil in a medium pot over medium-high heat. While whisking continuously, slowly sprinkle in the grits. Add ½ teaspoon salt and ½ teaspoon black pepper. When the grits begin to bubble, reduce the heat to low and cook, whisking occasionally, until thickened, 15 to 20 minutes. Remove from the heat and whisk in the cheese and butter until melted. Cover with a lid to keep warm until ready to serve.

Make the shrimp: In a cast-iron skillet, heat the oil over medium-high heat. Add the garlic and cook, stirring occasionally, until fragrant, about 2 minutes. Add the wine to the pan and bring to a boil. Reduce the heat to medium-low and cook until the wine has reduced by half, about 2 minutes. Add the shrimp, salt, black pepper, and chicken stock and simmer until the shrimp are pink and tender, about 4 minutes.

Add the butter, lemon juice, and hot sauce and swirl the pan, allowing butter to melt. Shut off the heat and add the cayenne and parsley to finish, then season lightly with salt to taste.

Uncover the grits and whisk in more stock or milk to reach your desired consistency. Ladle the grits onto a plate and top with the shrimp and sauce. Enjoy!

CORNFLAKE-CRUSTED FRIED GREEN TOMATOES WITH CHIPOTLE RANCH

SERVES 10 **PREP TIME** 15 MINUTES **TOTAL TIME** 30 MINUTES

1 cup buttermilk

1 large egg, lightly beaten

1 garlic clove, finely grated

Kosher salt and freshly ground black pepper

2 unripe green tomatoes, sliced ½ inch thick

2 cups crushed cornflakes

1 cup all-purpose flour

2 teaspoons garlic powder

1 teaspoon smoked paprika

¼ teaspoon cayenne pepper

Vegetable oil, for frying

1 cup Ranch Sauce (see page 120)

1 canned chipotle pepper in adobo sauce

My dad talked about his mom's fried green tomatoes ALL.THE.TIME. like they were the best thing since sliced bread. And I believe they were, even though I never had the privilege of knowing his mom or tasting her food. Because she was the matriarch who paved the way for soul food in my family, I had to do this recipe justice. Fried green tomatoes with cheese grits is a traditional Southern breakfast, though you could enjoy these any time of day. BTW, whoever came up with the idea to coat green tomatoes in breadcrumbs and fry them was a freakin' genius!! And thank God for that genius, or we would all be lost. We're using cornflakes instead of breadcrumbs to crust it up. Why? Because we can.

In a wide shallow dish, whisk together the buttermilk, egg, garlic, ½ teaspoon salt, and ¼ teaspoon black pepper. Add the tomato slices and turn to coat both sides. Soak the slices for 10 minutes, turning them halfway through.

In another shallow dish, mix together the cornflakes, flour, garlic powder, paprika, cayenne, 1 teaspoon salt, and ½ teaspoon black pepper. Set aside.

Line a rimmed baking sheet with aluminum foil and set a wire rack on top.

Heat 2 inches of oil in a cast-iron skillet over medium-high heat until shimmering. Remove the tomatoes from the buttermilk mixture, letting any excess drip off, and coat the tomatoes in the cornflakes, pressing so that the crumbs adhere to the tomatoes. Using tongs, add the tomatoes to the hot oil and fry until golden brown on both sides, 1 to 2 minutes per side. Drain on the prepared rack and hit with more salt.

In a blender, combine the ranch sauce and chipotle and blend until smooth. Serve alongside the fried green tomatoes.

YOU BETTER PIMIENTO POBLANO YOUR CORN CAKES

MAKES 16 TO 20 CORN CAKES   **PREP TIME** 15 MINUTES   **TOTAL TIME** 30 MINUTES

2 medium poblano peppers

1½ cups yellow cornmeal

1¾ teaspoons baking powder

½ teaspoon kosher salt

¼ teaspoon chili powder

⅔ cup buttermilk

3 large eggs

5 tablespoons unsalted butter, melted and cooled, plus more for serving

2 tablespoons honey, plus more for serving

½ cup Pimiento Cheese Spread (see page 123)

Sour cream, for serving

2 tablespoons chopped fresh flat-leaf parsley (optional)

These hot corn griddle cakes should be sold on every street corner in the world. There is no better way to wake up your hungover friends for brunch than with the smell of "something" burning. And by "something," I mean poblano peppers, of course. Burning anything feels like some sort of letting-go and spiritual ritual. Poblano peppers have not fulfilled their destiny until they have been thrown onto fire, blistered up, and achieved that notorious smoky flavor. I was first introduced to poblano peppers in high school when a classmate brought her mother's chiles rellenos for lunch; I nearly died at the smell—it was so good! I never got to taste the dish, but I could not get the smell out of my head. Roasted poblanos and corn are a classic Mexican combo, so it was obvious to me they would work well in this recipe. These corn cakes are the perfect marriage of a pancake and a slab of cornbread in one bite. The pimiento cheese spread gives these babies a creamy, salty bite. The honey and sour cream finish this game out on a win. If you need more convincing to try them out, shame on you!

Roast the poblano peppers over a gas stovetop burner on medium-high heat, rotating them frequently with tongs, until the skin is black all over, 3 to 4 minutes. Transfer the peppers to a heatproof bowl and cover bowl with plastic wrap or a kitchen towel for 2 minutes. Run the peppers under cold water and gently rub the skin to remove it; discard the skin. Discard the seeds and stem, and finely chop the peppers' flesh.

RECIPE CONTINUES ≫

In a medium bowl, whisk together the cornmeal, baking powder, salt, and chili powder. Whisk in the buttermilk, eggs, 4 table-spoons of the butter, and the honey. Fold in the chopped roasted pepper and pimiento cheese spread and mix until smooth.

Heat the remaining 1 tablespoon butter in a large cast-iron skillet over medium heat. Working in batches to avoid crowding the pan, drop ¼-cup portions of the batter into the pan. Cook until browned on the bottom and bubbling around the edges, 2 to 3 minutes. Using a spatula, flip the corn cakes and cook until golden brown on the other side, about 1 minute more. Repeat with the remaining batter.

Serve with butter, honey, and a dollop of sour cream and garnish with the parsley.

THE GRAVY

If, for whatever reason, you can't get ahold of poblano peppers, use a green bell pepper.

NYC BAGEL FRENCH TOAST PUDDING WITH BLUEBERRY CRUMBLE

SERVES 10 TO 12 **PREP TIME** 5 MINUTES **TOTAL TIME** 40 MINUTES

6 tablespoons (¾ stick) unsalted butter, at room temperature

¼ cup plus 1 tablespoon granulated sugar

1 tablespoon plus ¼ teaspoon ground cinnamon

4 cinnamon raisin bagels, cut into 1-inch cubes

6 large eggs

2 cups heavy cream

1 teaspoon vanilla extract

¼ teaspoon freshly grated nutmeg

Pinch of kosher salt

½ cup packed light brown sugar

½ cup all-purpose flour

1 pint fresh blueberries

Maple syrup, hot, for serving

NYC is home of the bagels. In Queens alone, they're maybe 1,000 bagel trucks selling you guessed it. Apparently, what makes NYC bagels so good are our water quality and horrible air quality. Fun fact: Did you know it takes more than a billion gallons of water to quench 9 million New Yorkers daily? I just Googled it. Are we thirsty or what?! I digress. The half dozen eggs and pint of heavy cream put the *French* in this toast. This is a make-ahead recipe that feeds an army. The blueberry crumble topping alone makes it worth making this dish.

Preheat the oven to 350°F. Butter a 9 x 13-inch casserole dish with 2 tablespoons of the butter.

In a small bowl, combine the granulated sugar and 1 tablespoon of the cinnamon. Sprinkle the bottom of the prepared dish with 2 teaspoons of the cinnamon-sugar mixture. Place the bagel pieces evenly in the prepared casserole dish.

In a large bowl, whisk together the eggs, cream, vanilla, nutmeg, salt, and remaining cinnamon-sugar mixture until frothy. Pour over the bagel pieces to coat evenly. Using your hands or a spoon, press down the bagel pieces to fully submerge in the egg mixture. Set aside.

In a medium bowl, use your hands to combine the brown sugar, flour, and remaining ¼ teaspoon cinnamon. Work the remaining 4 tablespoons butter in using your hands and mix until it forms coarse crumbs. Stir in the blueberries. Sprinkle the blueberry topping over the casserole and bake until the custard is set and the top is golden brown, 35 to 40 minutes. Let it sit for about 10 minutes before serving.

Serve warm with hot maple syrup.

AUNT JEMIMA'S APPLE PIE PANCAKES

SERVES 8 TO 10 **PREP TIME** 10 MINUTES **TOTAL TIME** 25 MINUTES

APPLE COMPOTE

3 tablespoons unsalted butter

1 Granny Smith apple, peeled, cored, and medium diced

2 Golden Delicious apples, peeled, cored, and medium diced

½ cup packed light brown sugar

1 teaspoon apple pie spice

2 teaspoons fresh lemon juice

Kosher salt

PANCAKES

1 cup Aunt Jemima pancake mix

¾ cup whole milk

⅓ cup chopped walnuts (optional)

2 teaspoons pure vanilla extract

1 teaspoon apple pie spice

Unsalted butter, for the pan

Confectioners' sugar, for dusting

Listen, I can't knock Aunt Jemima. She's been holding me and my family down for years. I think there are many lazy cooks out there who don't care to measure out a bunch of ingredients. Instead, they would rather jazz up a box of Aunt Jemima's. I don't blame you. I got you. For this recipe, no water. Use milk instead. Add some vanilla and cinnamon for some extra bong-bong. Dice up some apples, toss them in a pan with brown sugar, butter, and cinnamon, and make a sauce. Pour that over your pancakes, and voilà—life deserves a party! My cousins in London go bananas—or, should I say, go apples—for Aunt Jemima.

Make the apple compote: Melt the butter in a 10-inch skillet over medium heat. Stir in the apples, brown sugar, apple pie spice, lemon juice, and ¼ cup water. Cook, stirring occasionally, until the apples are slightly softened and the sauce is bubbling, 10 to 12 minutes. Sprinkle lightly with salt. Keep warm over low heat until ready to serve. (Alternatively, you can make the apple compote 3 days ahead and store in the refrigerator and reheat over low heat just before serving.)

Make the pancakes: In a large bowl, whisk together the pancake mix, milk, walnuts (if using), vanilla, and apple pie spice until just combined. Keep dem lumps!

Brush a large flat-top griddle or wide skillet with some butter and heat over medium heat until the surface is hot, about 2 minutes. Working in batches to avoid crowding the pan, drop ¼-cup portions of the batter onto the griddle and cook until the pancakes are lightly browned on one side, 3 to 4 minutes. Flip and cook until golden brown on the other side, about 2 minutes more. Transfer the pancakes to a plate and tent them with aluminum foil to keep them warm. Repeat with the remaining batter, brushing the griddle with butter as needed between batches.

Serve warm with the apple compote and confectioners' sugar.

MAPLE SYRUP <u>AND</u> SRIRACHA–GLAZED BACON

SERVES 6 **PREP TIME** 5 MINUTES **TOTAL TIME** 45 MINUTES

1 pound thick-cut bacon (about 12 slices)

¼ cup pure maple syrup

2 tablespoons Sriracha

This bacon is seriously dangerous! You can bite off your fingers eating it, it's that good! Bacon is a lifestyle. You don't just cook bacon and forget about it. It goes with you everywhere, perfumes you and your home from head to toe. Whenever you cook bacon, everyone on your block should know. I'm not sure what inspired this recipe more: my love for bacon, or my love for Sriracha anything. I pretty much love bacon and Sriracha for all the same reasons: They raise my blood pressure, increase my sodium levels, and force me to go back for more. You could also do this with pork belly . . . ooo la la. No fakin' here.

Place oven racks in the upper and lower thirds of the oven. Preheat the oven to 375°F. Line a baking sheet with two layers of aluminum foil and set a wire rack on top.

Arrange the bacon slices on the wire rack in a single layer. Set aside.

In a small bowl, mix together the maple syrup and Sriracha. Spoon 2 tablespoons into a separate small bowl and set aside. Brush the top of the bacon with half of the remaining glaze. Cook the bacon in the oven until the top is crisp, about 30 minutes. Flip the bacon and glaze with the remaining glaze. Cook until crisp, 20 to 25 minutes more. Remove from the oven.

Brush the bacon with the reserved 2 tablespoons glaze and serve.

EGG-AND-CHEESE SCRAMBLE ON A BISCUIT

SERVES 4 **PREP TIME** 15 MINUTES **TOTAL TIME** 25 MINUTES

BISCUITS

2 cups all-purpose flour

1½ tablespoons sugar

1 tablespoon baking powder

1 teaspoon kosher salt

½ cup (1 stick) unsalted butter or shortening, cut into cubes and chilled, plus melted butter for brushing

¾ cup buttermilk

SCRAMBLE

6 large eggs

Freshly ground black pepper

4 slices salami, chopped

½ cup shredded Monterey Jack cheese

1 tablespoon chopped fresh chives, for serving

You're not really a New Yorker if you've never had a bacon, egg, and cheese from a bodega. And not just any bodega—I mean the ones where cats are the bodyguards. To think I used to eat them all the time with a bottle of Hawaiian Punch scares me. This book would not be complete without an egg-and-cheese on a biscuit. My egg-and-cheese scramble must be cooked gently over medium-low heat and stirred often to achieve that creamy, soft texture. The flaky biscuits replace the greasy deli buttered roll (which I do have love for. I do.). This is a glutton's choice breakfast. A breakfast for champs. I'm counted among them. And, of course, I eat this every day—you should, too!

Make the biscuits: Preheat the oven to 425°F. Line a large baking sheet with parchment paper.

In the bowl of a food processor, combine the flour, sugar, baking powder, and salt. Add the cold butter and pulse about twelve times (you want to see small pieces of butter throughout the mixture). Pulse in the buttermilk until the mixture is well combined and forms a dough, about 15 seconds.

Transfer the dough to a lightly floured work surface. Using lightly floured hands, pat the dough out into a 7 x 5-inch rectangle, 1 inch thick. Cut out 4 biscuits using a 2½- to 3-inch-diameter biscuit cutter. Transfer biscuits and dough scraps to the prepared baking sheet. Brush tops of the biscuits and scraps with some melted butter and bake until golden brown, about 15 minutes. Brush the finished biscuits with additional melted butter.

RECIPE CONTINUES ⟫⟫

THE GRAVY

Whenever you use a nonstick skillet, use a rubber spatula or gentle cooking tool to stir ingredients to prevent scratching off the nonstick surface.

Make the scramble: In a large bowl, whisk together the eggs and black pepper. Set aside.

In a dry nonstick skillet, cook the salami over medium heat, stirring occasionally, until crisp, about 3 minutes. Reduce the heat to low and add the eggs. Cook, stirring often, until the eggs are just firm but still creamy, about 3 minutes. Stir in the cheese and cook until the cheese has melted and the eggs are set, about 2 minutes more.

Slice the biscuits in half crosswise and divide the eggs evenly among the biscuits. Garnish with the chives and serve immediately.

NUTELLA BACON BANANA BREAKFAST GRILLED CHEESE!
WHOA!

SERVES 2 **PREP TIME** 10 MINUTES **TOTAL TIME** 25 MINUTES

- 8 thick-cut slices bacon, halved crosswise
- 4 tablespoons (½ stick) unsalted butter, at room temperature
- 8 slices Pepperidge Farm Chocolatey Chip Swirl or Cinnamon Swirl bread
- ½ cup mascarpone cheese
- ½ cup Nutella
- 2 bananas, sliced

There's a dope grilled cheese spot in Buffalo, New York, called Melting Point. They close at 2 a.m. for obvious reasons. The No. 50 is probably my personal favorite on the menu. It's ricotta, candied bacon, Nutella, and banana on cinnamon swirl bread. It's a crazy combo. I've come up with my own version using their template—mascarpone instead of ricotta, regular bacon instead of candied, and chocolate swirl bread instead of cinnamon swirl. This is the most insane grilled cheese you will ever eat . . . ever. Also, this is just another excuse to eat Nutella ☺.

In a large cast-iron skillet, cook the bacon over medium heat until crisp, about 4 minutes on each side. Remove the bacon from the skillet and drain on a paper towel–lined plate. Drain the remaining fat from the skillet and wipe with a paper towel.

Butter one side of each slice of bread. Place the bread on a work surface, buttered-side down. Spread the mascarpone cheese evenly over the unbuttered sides of half the bread slices. Spread the Nutella on the remaining bread slices. Add 4 pieces of bacon and the banana slices to each Nutella-topped slice of bread. Top with the mascarpone-topped slices to form sandwiches.

Working in batches, cook the sandwiches in a cast-iron skillet over medium heat until golden brown on one side, about 3 minutes. Flip the sandwiches and cook until golden on the other side, about 3 minutes more. Remove the grilled cheese from the skillet, slice it in half, and serve.

THE GRAVY

Mascarpone cheese is an Italian cream cheese. It tastes like sour cream and cream cheese made a baby.

I'M A ROCKSTAR CHEF. I LIKE THE SPICE, THE TANG, AND THE SALTY. I LIKE THE HEAT AND THE SWEET, THE BOLD AND THE SUBTLE. I LIKE VARIETY, PLAYS ON TEMPERATURE AND TEXTURE. I LIKE THE FUNKY AND THE FRESH, THE SOPHISTICATED AND THE SIMPLE. IT'S ALL GRAVY IN MY WORLD, AND WELCOME IN MY KITCHEN ANYTIME.

—Lazarus Lynch

SAVAGE SCHNACKS

THE GRAVY

Let's talk guac for a second. I like a chunky guac. Lemme see that avo, dem tomatoes, and that red onion. When choosing avocados, look for firm to the touch but not rock hard. They should give slightly when squeezed but should never feel like a baseball.

LOADED SHORT RIB NACHOS

SERVES 6 TO 8 **PREP TIME** 10 MINUTES **TOTAL TIME** 8 HOURS 20 MINUTES

SHORT RIBS

1 pound short ribs

1 teaspoon sweet paprika

½ teaspoon garlic powder

Kosher salt and freshly ground black pepper

3 teapoons canola oil

¾ cup ketchup

2 tablespoons packed light brown sugar

1 tablespoon yellow mustard

2 teaspoons Worcestershire sauce

2 teaspoons apple cider vinegar

BASIC GUAC

2 ready-to-go avocados

1 Roma (plum) tomato, diced

¼ cup chopped red onion

2 tablespoons chopped fresh cilantro

2 tablespoons fresh lime juice

½ teaspoon kosher salt

¼ teaspoon freshly ground black pepper

TO SERVE

Tortilla chips

¾ cup shredded Monterey Jack cheese

I am a sucker for short ribs anything. I'm also a sucker for salty nachos covered in hot, processed yellow cheese sauce, like the kind you get at the movies. But when I make a loaded nachos for myself, I start with the basics: guac, salsa, red onion, sour cream, shredded cheese, and, of course, my short ribs! The best part of this dish is the sunken chips at the bottom that absorb the BBQ juice like a sponge. You could straight up Netflix and chill with a plate of these on your lap. I'm very guilty.

Make the short ribs: Pat the short ribs dry with a paper towel and season with the paprika, garlic, 1 teaspoon salt, and ½ teaspoon pepper.

Heat the oil in a large skillet over high heat until almost smoking. Working in batches, cook the short ribs, turning occasionally, until browned on all sides, 8 to 10 minutes.

Place the short ribs in a slow cooker with the ketchup, brown sugar, mustard, Worcestershire, vinegar, and ¼ cup water. Cover and cook on low for 8 hours, or until the ribs are extremely tender. Remove the ribs from the slow cooker and shred the rib meat from the bones using two forks. Drain any excess fat from the sauce in the slow cooker and return the meat to the sauce.

Make the guac: Peel the avocados, remove the pit, and mash the flesh in a medium bowl. Mix in the tomato, onion, cilantro, lime juice, salt, and pepper.

To serve: Place the tortilla chips on a large serving platter and top with the guac and pulled short ribs, then make it rain with the cheese. Alternatively, individually plate the nachos on six to eight appetizer plates.

GUYANESE CHEESE ROLLS

MAKES 12 ROLLS **PREP TIME** 10 MINUTES **TOTAL TIME** 40 MINUTES

2 cups grated sharp cheddar cheese

¼ cup yellow mustard

1 tablespoon chopped fresh rosemary

2 teaspoons garlic powder

1 to 2 teaspoons Red Hot Pepper Sauce (page 204)

1 teaspoon freshly ground black pepper

1 large egg

1 package (2 sheets) frozen puff pastry, such as Pepperidge Farm, thawed

There's a cool Guyanese bakery in my hood called Sybil's Bakery NYC that sells these amazing cheese rolls. They are perfection. My mom worked at a nearby hospital back in the day, and Sybil's became our pull-up spot. I've managed to re-create these cheese rolls (MY WAY), and I think they're just as delicious as the ones from the Guyanese bakeries. These taste dope by themselves but they're even better when dunked in some mango chutney (page 194), or my hot sauce, or both!

Preheat the oven to 450°F. Line a baking sheet with parchment paper.

In a medium bowl, mix together the cheese, mustard, rosemary, garlic powder, hot pepper sauce, and black pepper.

In a separate small bowl, beat together the egg and 1 tablespoon water for the egg wash.

On a floured surface, roll one sheet of the puff pastry into a 10 x 12-inch rectangle. Place the cheese filling in the center of the pastry and spread it out into an even layer, leaving a 1-inch border. Fold the dough into thirds, overlapping the layers like a letter, and slice it into 6 rectangular pieces, about 4 inches long by 1½ inches wide. Transfer the pastries to the prepared baking sheet and brush them with half the egg wash. Repeat with the second puff pastry sheet.

Bake until golden brown and puffy, 20 to 25 minutes. Serve warm.

RED HOT PEPPER SAUCE
(page 204)

CURRY CHICKEN PATTIES

MAKES 12 PATTIES   **PREP TIME** 20 MINUTES   **TOTAL TIME** 1 HOUR

2 tablespoons canola oil

½ yellow onion, finely chopped

½ red bell pepper, finely chopped

2 garlic cloves, minced

2 scallions, finely chopped

1 tablespoon fresh thyme

¾ pound ground chicken

1 tablespoon plus 2 teaspoons Jamaican-style yellow curry powder

½ teaspoon ground cumin

Kosher salt and freshly ground black pepper

1 tablespoon tomato paste

2 teaspoons Red Hot Pepper Sauce (page 204), plus more for serving

1 large egg

1 package (2 sheets) frozen puff pastry, such as Pepperidge Farm, thawed

This is a tribute to my obsession with Jamaican beef patties! I remember dipping into my dad's cash register at his restaurant and racing around the corner for some patties. I'm using chicken for this recipe, but you could also use ground beef or ground turkey. I will say, these patties go quickly with my family, so making a few extra isn't a bad idea.

Preheat the oven to 400°F. Line a large baking sheet with parchment paper.

Heat the oil in a large skillet over medium-high heat. Add the onion, bell pepper, garlic, scallions, and thyme and cook, stirring occasionally, until lightly browned and tender, about 5 minutes. Add the chicken, 1 tablespoon of the curry powder, and the cumin and cook, stirring with a wooden spoon, until evenly browned, about 10 minutes. Add 1½ teaspoons salt and ¼ teaspoon black pepper, then stir in the tomato paste and hot pepper sauce. Cook for 2 minutes.

In a small bowl, whisk together the egg, 1 tablespoon water, and remaining 2 teaspoons curry powder to make the egg wash.

On a floured surface, unfold the puff pastry and cut into 4-inch rounds. Fill each round with 1 heaping tablespoon of the filling, leaving a ½-inch border. Brush the edges with the egg wash, fold the pastry in half over the filling, and crimp the edges with a fork to seal.

Place the pastries on the prepared baking sheet. Brush with the egg wash and bake until golden, 20 to 22 minutes. Transfer to a wire rack and let cool slightly before serving.

Serve with additional hot pepper sauce alongside.

BUFFALO CHICKEN BLUE LOLLIPOPS

SERVES 12 **PREP TIME** 15 MINUTES **TOTAL TIME** 50 MINUTES

½ cup your favorite hot sauce

2 tablespoons unsalted butter, melted and cooled slightly

Two (6-ounce) chicken breasts, cut into 24 bite-size pieces

12 slices bacon, halved crosswise

1 cup crumbled blue cheese

½ cup sour cream

¼ cup mayonnaise

Celery and carrot sticks, for serving (optional)

I am the sum of all the places I have lived and foods I have tasted. I went to college in Buffalo, New York, home to Anchor Bar and Duff's Famous Wings. I must admit, I was not a huge Buffalo wing/sauce person before moving to Buffalo, but now I'm a fan! My favorite part of this recipe is dunking (sometimes double-dunking) these lollipops in the blue cheese dressing. Okay, I'm sharing too much.

Preheat the oven to 425°F. Line a baking sheet with two sheets of heavy-duty luminum foil and set a wire rack on top.

In a large bowl, mix together the hot sauce and the melted butter. Set aside ¼ cup of the hot sauce mixture, then add the chicken to the remainder and toss well to coat. Lay the bacon out on a clean work surface and top each piece with one piece of chicken. Sprinkle ½ cup of the blue cheese over the chicken. Wrap the bacon over the filling tightly and secure with a toothpick. Place seam-side down on the wire rack. Bake until the bacon is crisp and sizzling, about 25 minutes. Brush the lollipops with the remaining hot sauce mixture. Flip the lollipops over and bake until crisp, about 20 minutes more.

Meanwhile, in a small bowl, whisk together the remaining ½ cup blue cheese, the sour cream, and the mayonnaise until smooth.

Transfer the chicken lollipops to a plate and serve with the blue cheese dressing and celery and carrot sticks, if desired.

THE GRAVY

Avoid cross-contamination by washing hands thoroughly after handling raw meat and keeping the carrots and celery separate from the uncooked lollipops until ready to serve.

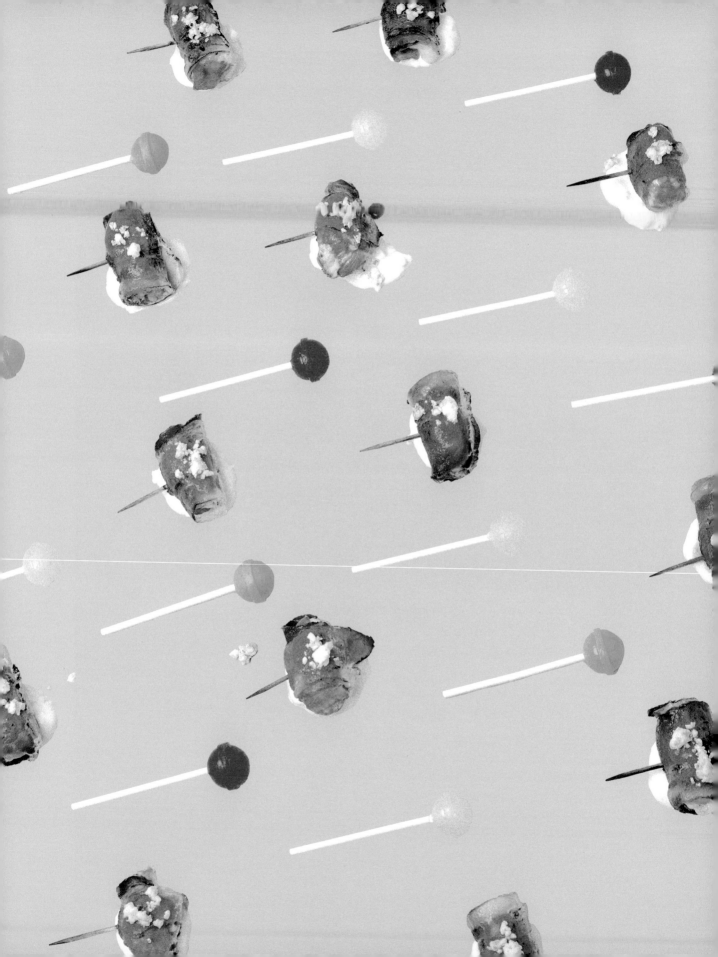

GREEN DEVILED EGGS AND HAM

MAKES 12 DEVILED EGGS   **PREP TIME** 15 MINUTES   **TOTAL TIME** 25 MINUTES

6 large eggs

1 Hass avocado, pitted and peeled

2 tablespoons tender fresh herb leaves, such as flat-leaf parsley, dill, or chives

1 teaspoon fresh lemon juice

½ teaspoon Dijon mustard

Splash of your favorite hot sauce

Pinch salt

Pinch freshly ground black pepper

2 thin slices country ham (about ½ ounce), chopped

¼ cup chopped pickled jalapeños (optional)

Who has not read or heard of Dr. Seuss's *Green Eggs and Ham*? This recipe is completely inspired by that classic book. I think Dr. Seuss was a genius way ahead of his time to imagine this wacky food combo, but it actually works. The "green" comes from mixing the yolks with avo and herbs, and the "ham" part is crispy deli ham. A good deviled egg, to me, is made with a perfectly cooked hard-boiled egg, and has the right ratio of filling to egg white. I also love serving these with finely chopped pickled jalapeños or pickles. These are green eggs and ham, Son of a Southern Chef style.

Bring 2 quarts water to a boil in a large saucepan. Add the eggs and cook for 13 minutes. Shut off heat and cover the saucepan for 3 minutes more. Drain the eggs and cool under cold running water. Gently tap the eggs on a flat surface and peel the eggs. Rinse off any remaining eggshells and halve lengthwise.

Scoop out the yolks and put them in a mini food processor along with the avocado, herbs, lemon juice, Dijon, hot sauce, salt, and pepper. Process until very smooth. Season lightly with salt and pepper. Transfer the filling to a pastry bag or a plastic zip-top bag with ½ inch snipped off a bottom corner to make a small opening. Fill the egg whites with the filling. Top with the chopped ham, then the pickled jalapeños, and serve.

THE GRAVY

"Deviled" is a Southern term that means "heavily spiced or seasoned." It does not mean this recipe came from the devil, LOL. The eggs can be cooked a day in advance.

CORN AND GREEN ONION FRITTERS

WITH *Red Pepper Comeback Sauce*

SERVES 6 **PREP TIME** 10 MINUTES **TOTAL TIME** 25 MINUTES

2 teaspoons olive oil

1 cup fresh or thawed frozen corn kernels

1 large garlic clove, minced

½ cup all-purpose flour

½ teaspoon baking powder

½ teaspoon kosher salt

Pinch cayenne pepper

½ cup buttermilk

1 large egg white

¼ cup freshly grated Parmesan cheese

2 scallions, green parts only, finely chopped

Canola oil, for frying

Flaky salt, such as Maldon sea salt flakes, for serving

Red Pepper Comeback Sauce (recipe follows), for serving

Corn fritters are so underrated, IMO. Fritter anything, I am sold. These fritters come together so quickly, and the ingredients are highly accessible. Usually, I have most of the ingredients on deck in my pantry, minus the fresh corn. These fritters were a hit the first time I made them, and the Comeback Sauce is DOPE! This recipe makes more sauce than is needed for this recipe—I considered cutting the recipe in half, but I didn't, and you'll thank me when you taste it. It's called "comeback" for a reason, LOL!

Heat the olive oil in a medium skillet over medium-high heat. Add the corn and garlic and cook, stirring occasionally, until softened and fragrant, 3 to 4 minutes. Turn off the heat and set aside.

In a separate bowl, mix together the flour, baking powder, salt, and cayenne. Whisk the buttermilk and egg white into the flour mixture and fold in the cooked corn mixture, Parmesan, and scallions.

Heat 3 inches of canola oil in a large pot or Dutch oven over medium-high heat until it registers 365°F on a candy thermometer. Carefully drop 1 tablespoon of the fritter batter into the hot oil and repeat with as much batter as you can without overcrowding. Fry until golden brown on all sides, turning the fritters occasionally, about 5 minutes. Use a slotted spoon to transfer the fritters to a paper towel–lined plate and season immediately with flaky salt. Repeat with the remaining batter, adjusting the temperature of the oil as needed.

Serve the fritters with this dope Red Pepper Comeback Sauce.

RED PEPPER COMEBACK SAUCE

MAKES 1 CUP

One (4-ounce) jar sliced pimientos, drained and patted dry

½ cup mayonnaise

1 scallion, green part only, finely chopped

2 teaspoons smoked paprika

2 teaspoons fresh lemon juice or white vinegar

1 teaspoon Dijon mustard

1 small garlic clove

½ teaspoon kosher salt

Pinch cayenne pepper

In a small food processor, blitz together the pimientos, mayonnaise, scallion, paprika, lemon juice, Dijon, garlic, salt, and cayenne until smooth. Serve immediately or store in an airtight container in the fridge for up to 5 days.

BOILED PEANUTS WITH SMOKED SALT

SERVES 4 **PREP TIME** 5 MINUTES **TOTAL TIME** 7 HOURS

1 pound raw peanuts in the shell

2 tablespoons Maldon smoked sea salt

1 tablespoon chili powder

1 tablespoon hot smoked paprika

1 tablespoon light or dark brown sugar

1 large garlic clove, smashed

½ teaspoon cayenne pepper

Who boils peanuts? Who snacks on boiled peanuts? These are valid questions, particularly of non-Southerners. One of my fondest memories of Dad was watching him boil peanuts in a huge pot for hours and hours, then he devoured them. A true Southerner would agree that boiled peanuts are not only stupid-good, but they surprisingly taste nothing like a peanut once they're cooked. The peanuts are boiled whole in the shell, which transforms their texture. They taste more like a cooked bean, which is kinda nuts (no pun intended). If you drive through the back roads in the South, chances are you'll find a boiled peanut stand. I low-key spotted a peanut stand in my New York City neighborhood the other day and was immediately transported to the South. The next level is soaking the peanuts in pop (yean, I said "pop" like soda), then snacking. I top my peanuts with smoked salt for a barbecue vibe.

In a large pot or slow cooker, combine the peanuts, sea salt, chili powder, paprika, brown sugar, garlic, and cayenne and add water to cover. Cover and cook over high heat (or in the slow cooker on High) until the peanuts are very tender on the inside and float to the top, about 6 hours, adding water as necessary to keep the peanuts submerged. Adjust salt as desired.

Pour the peanuts and their cooking liquid into a heatproof container and let cool slightly, about 10 minutes.

Serve warm and top with more smoked salt. You can also refrigerate the peanuts in the brine in an airtight container for up to 2 days and reheat in a saucepan over medium-low heat to serve warm.

 THE GRAVY

Cooking time depends on the freshness of the peanuts. Fresher peanuts will take less time to cook. Fresh green peanuts take about 1 to 3 hours to cook. The longer the peanuts sit in the liquid, the saltier they get, so taste them as you go. If they are too salty, soak them in fresh water until they are as salty as you desire.

OLD BAY POTATO CHIPS

SERVES 6 **PREP TIME** 10 MINUTES **TOTAL TIME** 40 MINUTES

Peanut or vegetable oil
  for deep frying

2 tablespoons white vinegar

1 tablespoon kosher salt

1 tablespoon Old Bay
  seasoning, divided

2 medium russet potatoes
  (about 1¼ pounds),
  washed and dried

We are regular chip eaters in my household. My favorite chips growing up were UTZ Salt and Vinegar chips (who's with me?). I would literally lick the inner lining of the bag so I didn't waste a single crumb. I think every sandwich begs for a side of crispy potato chips (or a sorry kale salad). This is your basic potato chip recipe, and I finish them with Old Bay seasoning. You can sprinkle them with whatever fairy dust flavor you like and make them your own.

Fill a Dutch oven or heavy-bottomed pot with oil to a depth of 3 inches and heat over medium-high heat to 375°F, about 10 minutes. Fill a large pot or bucket with 1 gallon water, the vinegar, salt, and ½ tablespoon of the Old Bay seasoning.

Using a mandoline or sharp vegetable peeler, slice potatoes very thin (about ⅛ inch thick). Watch your fingers. Soak the sliced potatoes in the water solution as you continue to slice to keep them from browning.

Drain the potatoes, transfer to a paper towel–lined baking tray, and pat dry with additional paper towel. Line a second tray or large bowl with fresh paper towel. Working in small batches, carefully drop them into the hot oil and fry until golden and crispy, 2 to 3 minutes. Transfer the chips to a tray or bowl and hit them with the remaining Old Bay seasoning. Repeat with the remaining potatoes, letting the temperature of the oil return to 375°F between each fry.

Transfer to a bowl and serve immediately.

CRISPY ESCOVITCH
FISH (page 231)

WATERMELON
WITH LIME, CHILE, <u>AND</u> SALT

SERVES 4 TO 6   **PREP TIME** 10 MINUTES   **TOTAL TIME** 10 MINUTES

Zest and juice of 5 limes

2 tablespoons chipotle chili powder

2 teaspoons fine sea salt

Juice of 2 large oranges

One (3-pound) seedless watermelon, sliced into wedges

⅓ cup fresh mint leaves, torn

There's no Southern politeness to my watermelon-eatin'. The juice runs down my arms, down to my elbows, and my shirt becomes a bib. This is the proper way to eat watermelon. I imagine my folks back in the day sitting on their wooden porches slicing up watermelon on a hot Sunday after church and calling out to my dad, *"Hey Lil' Johnny, bring us some hot sauce."* I crave a juicy slice in the hot summer months with a pinch of sea salt, lime, and chipotle chili powder to bring out all that sweet. Though it's great in the summer, I'm in the mood for this schnack all year-round.

In a small bowl, mix together the lime zest, chili powder, and salt. Pour the lime juice and orange juice over the watermelon and sprinkle with the salt mixture. Garnish with the mint leaves.

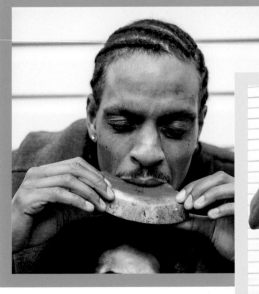

FRIED OKRA "WHOLE"

SERVES 8 TO 12   **PREP TIME** 5 MINUTES   **TOTAL TIME** 30 MINUTES

Canola oil, for frying

¾ cup buttermilk

1 cup self-rising flour

½ cup yellow cornmeal

1 tablespoon sweet paprika

1 tablespoon garlic powder

2 teaspoons cayenne pepper

Kosher salt and freshly
  ground black pepper

1 pound fresh whole okra

Lemon wedges, for serving
  (optional)

Your favorite hot sauce,
  for serving

Have you ever seen the crowd goin' APES**T? People flipped out on social media when I first posted this recipe. Apparently, no one fries okra whole, but I didn't get the memo. When okra gets fried in my household, literally, the entire house comes alive at the aroma. At the restaurant, Dad used Old Bay and adobo with garlic to season his fried okra. Once they were cooked, he would sprinkle a bit more Old Bay on top and serve hot. Frying okra still gets my house hype. It's litty!

Fill a Dutch oven or heavy-bottomed pot with oil to a depth of 3 inches and heat over medium heat to 360°F. Line a baking sheet with paper towels and set it nearby.

Pour the buttermilk into a shallow dish. In a large bowl, combine the flour, cornmeal, paprika, garlic powder, and cayenne and season with 2 teaspoons salt and 1 teaspoon black pepper.

Dip the okra in the buttermilk to coat completely. Allow the excess to drip off, then toss the okra in the flour mixture and place it in the hot oil. Working in batches, fry the okra, turning occasionally to cook evenly on all sides, for 2 to 3 minutes total, until golden brown. Transfer to the prepared baking sheet. Repeat until all the okra is cooked. Lightly season with salt.

Serve with lemon wedges, if desired, and your favorite hot sauce (YASSS!).

PICKLED THINGS

I freakin' LOVE pickles! Quick pickles are my favorite because they take no time at all to make. Here is everything you want to know about pickles in one succinct section.

For quick pickling, I like using 1-quart or 1-pint mason jars that are cleaned and dry.

HOUSE PICKLES
⌄⌄

PICKLED
CAULIFLOWER
⌄⌄

PICKLED
RED ONION
⌄⌄

PICKLED
CARROTS
⌄⌄

PICKLED
PEACHES
»

PICKLED
BEETS
»

PICKLED
RADISHES
»

PICKLED
GREEN BEANS
»

THE GRAVY

Trim the beet greens from the top of the beets,
wrap them in a damp paper towel, and store
in a zip-top bag for later use. You can cook
them like any other dark leafy green.

PICKLED CARROTS

MAKES 1 PINT
PREP TIME: 5 MINUTES
TOTAL TIME: 10 MINUTES

1 pound small tricolored carrots, trimmed

1 teaspoon coriander seeds

1 teaspoon fennel seeds

½ cup apple cider vinegar

3 tablespoons sugar

2 teaspoons kosher or pickling salt

1 teaspoon whole black peppercorns

One (1-inch) piece orange peel (peeled with a vegetable peeler)

Place the carrots in a clean and dry 1-pint mason jar. Toast the coriander and fennel in a small saucepan over medium-high heat, shaking the pan often, until fragrant, about 45 seconds. Add the vinegar, sugar, salt, peppercorns, orange peel, and 2 cups water and bring to a boil, stirring to dissolve the sugar and salt, about 3 minutes. Pour over the carrots and let cool before sealing the jar. Store in the refrigerator for up to 1 month.

HOUSE PICKLES

MAKES 1 QUART
PREP TIME: 5 MINUTES
TOTAL TIME: 10 MINUTES

1 pound Kirby cucumbers, halved lengthwise

6 large sprigs fresh dill

2 teaspoons caraway seeds

½ cup white vinegar

1 tablespoon sugar

1 tablespoon kosher or pickling salt

1 teaspoon whole black peppercorns

2 garlic cloves, thinly sliced

Place the cucumbers and dill sprigs in a clean and dry 1-quart mason jar. Toast the caraway seeds in a small saucepan over medium-high heat, shaking often, until fragrant, about 45 seconds. Add the vinegar, sugar, salt, peppercorns, garlic, and 1 cup water and bring to a boil, stirring until the sugar and salt have dissolved, about 3 minutes. Pour the hot pickling liquid into the jar and let cool completely before sealing the jar. Store in the refrigerator for up to 1 month.

PICKLED GREEN BEANS

MAKES 1 PINT
PREP TIME: 5 MINUTES
TOTAL TIME: 10 MINUTES

½ pound fresh green beans

2 sprigs fresh dill

¼ cup white vinegar

1 teaspoon kosher or pickling salt

1 teaspoon sugar

Place the green beans and dill in a clean and dry 1-pint mason jar. In a small saucepan, combine the vinegar, salt, sugar, and ¾ cup water. Cook over medium-high heat, stirring, until the salt and sugar have dissolved, about 1 minute. Pour the pickling liquid into the jar and let cool completely before sealing the jar. Store in the refrigerator for up to 1 month.

PICKLED RED ONION

MAKES 1 PINT
PREP TIME: 5 MINUTES
TOTAL TIME: 10 MINUTES

1 large red onion, sliced into strips

¾ cup red wine vinegar

2 tablespoons sugar

2 teaspoons kosher or pickling salt

½ teaspoon crushed red pepper flakes

Place the onion in a clean and dry 1-pint mason jar. In a small saucepan, combine the vinegar, sugar, salt, red pepper flakes, and 1 cup water and bring to a boil, then cook, stirring, until the sugar has dissolved, about 2 minutes. Pour the hot liquid over the onion and let cool before sealing the jar. Store in the refrigerator for up to 1 week.

PICKLED BEETS

MAKES 1 PINT
PREP TIME: 5 MINUTES
TOTAL TIME: 15 MINUTES

2 large beets, peeled, cut into ½-inch cubes

4 sprigs fresh thyme

½ teaspoon caraway seeds

½ cup red wine vinegar

2 garlic cloves, thinly sliced

2 star anise pods

1 teaspoon sugar

½ teaspoon kosher or pickling salt

Place the beets and thyme in a clean and dry 1-pint mason jar. Toast the caraway seeds in a small saucepan over medium-high heat, shaking the pan often, until fragrant, about 30 seconds. Add the vinegar, garlic, star anise, sugar, salt, and ½ cup water and bring to a boil, stirring to dissolve the sugar and salt, about 2 minutes. Pour the solution over the beets and let cool completely before sealing the jar. Store in the refrigerator for up to 1 month.

PICKLED CAULIFLOWER

MAKES 1 PINT
PREP TIME: 5 MINUTES
TOTAL TIME: 10 MINUTES

½ pound cauliflower florets

2 sprigs fresh dill

½ cup red wine vinegar

2 teaspoons sugar

2 teaspoons kosher or pickling salt

1 teaspoon whole black peppercorns

Place the cauliflower and dill in a clean and dry 1-pint mason jar. In a small saucepan, combine the vinegar, sugar, salt, peppercorns, and 1 cup water and bring to a boil. Cook, stirring, until the sugar and salt have dissolved, about 1 minute. Pour the hot liquid over the cauliflower and let cool before sealing the jar. Store in the refrigerator for up to 1 month.

PICKLED RADISHES

MAKES 1 PINT
PREP TIME: 5 MINUTES
TOTAL TIME: 10 MINUTES

12 radishes, quartered

1 teaspoon coriander seeds

½ cup apple cider vinegar

1 tablespoon honey or sugar

1 teaspoon kosher or pickling salt

1 fresh bay leaf

Place the radishes in a clean and dry 1-pint mason jar. Toast the coriander seeds in a medium saucepan over medium-high heat, shaking the pan often, until fragrant, about 30 seconds. Add the vinegar, honey, salt, coriander seeds, bay leaf, and 1 cup water and bring to a boil, about 2 minutes. Pour the liquid over the radishes and let cool before sealing the jar. Store in the refrigerator for up to 1 month.

PICKLED PEACHES

MAKES 1 PINT
PREP TIME: 10 MINUTES
TOTAL TIME: 20 MINUTES

6 yellow ripe peaches, peeled, pitted, and sliced

1 cup apple cider vinegar

¾ cup sugar

4 whole cloves

1 cinnamon stick

1 teaspoon whole black peppercorns

Place the peaches in a clean and dry 1-pint mason jar. In a small saucepan, combine the vinegar, sugar, cloves, cinnamon, peppercorns, and 1 cup water and bring to a boil, then reduce the heat to low and simmer for 5 minutes. Strain the hot liquid over the peaches and let cool. Discard the cloves, cinnamon, and peppercorns and seal the jar. Store in the refrigerator for up to 1 month.

IF COOKING STRESSES YOU OUT,

THROW ON SOME BEYONCÉ,
START A DANCE PARTY,

POP A BOTTLE, THEN START
COOKING.

WHEN YOU TURN COOKING
INTO A PARTY,

THE STRESS CAN'T STAY.

—*Lazarus Lynch*

ISSA
DRINKS
WAVE

PEACH AND BOURBON SWEET TEA

SERVES 4 **PREP TIME** 5 MINUTES **TOTAL TIME** 20 MINUTES

4 black tea bags

4 peaches, peeled, pitted, and sliced

½ cup fresh lemon juice

4 ounces Jim Beam bourbon

2 ounces (¼ cup) Ginger Simple Syrup (recipe follows)

Ice, for serving

10 lemon slices, for garnish

Fresh mint leaves, for garnish

No drink says "Southern hospitality" more than sweet tea! Mine is pretty straightforward and classic.

In a large saucepan, bring 4 cups water to a boil. Shut off the heat, add the tea bags, and steep for 10 minutes. Discard the tea bags.

In the bowl of a food processor or blender, blitz the peaches until smooth. Pour the peach puree into the tea, then stir in the lemon juice, bourbon, and Ginger Simple Syrup. Cover and refrigerate until cool.

Fill four glasses with ice. Divide the sweet tea among the glasses and garnish with the lemon slices and mint leaves.

GINGER SIMPLE SYRUP

MAKES 1 CUP TOTAL TIME: 5 MINUTES

1 cup sugar

1 tablespoon grated fresh ginger

In a medium saucepan, combine the sugar, ginger, and 1 cup water and bring to a full boil over medium-high heat. Cook, stirring occasionally, until the sugar dissolves, about 3 minutes. Transfer to a heatproof container and let cool. Store in the refrigerator for up to 2 weeks.

I'VE BEEN DRINKING WATERMELON COCKTAILS

SERVES 2 **PREP TIME** 5 MINUTES **TOTAL TIME** 10 MINUTES

2 teaspoons kosher salt

2 teaspoons sugar

2 teaspoons chili powder

Zest of 1 lime, plus lime wedges for serving

2 cups fresh watermelon juice

4 ounces tequila

2 ounces fresh citrus juice (any combination of orange, lemon, and lime)

½ ounce agave nectar

1 bunch fresh basil leaves, plus more for garnish

1 bunch fresh mint leaves, plus more for garnish

1 small jalapeño, sliced and seeded, plus more for garnish

Ice

Queen Bey inspired this one—let us all bow down. I could see Jay-Z and Beyoncé sipping on these on Maui . . . Hello! #GOALS ♥ ♥ ♥

Mix together the salt, sugar, chili powder, and lime zest on a small, shallow plate. Use lime wedges to wet the rims of two glasses, then gently press the rims into the salt mixture to coat.

Fill a cocktail shaker with watermelon juice, tequila, citrus juice, agave, 3 leaves each of the basil and mint, and jalapeño. Add ice and shake well, until the outside of the shaker is cold, about 30 seconds.

Strain cocktail through a strainer and fill the prepared glasses with the watermelon cocktail. Garnish each with basil, mint, and jalapeño.

COCONUT AND ORANGE SLUSH

SERVES 2 **PREP TIME** 5 MINUTES **TOTAL TIME** 10 MINUTES

1 fresh coconut

1 cup coconut milk

1 cup orange juice

1 cup ice

¼ cup pure honey

2 ounces Bacardi rum

If you took me on a cruise to Jamaica and put me on a beach, this is what I'd be drinking. I'm already cruising in my mind . . .

Find the dark holes or "eyes" of the coconut at the stem end. Stick a screwdriver into whichever eye is most penetrable to release the water. Pour 1 cup of the coconut water into a bowl and set aside.

Hold the coconut with a towel in your nondominant hand. Using the back of a chef's knife or cleaver, tap on the coconut along the sides, turning as needed, until the coconut cracks open.

In a blender, mix the coconut milk, orange juice, ice, honey, and rum. Pour the slush into the coconut halves and serve each with a straw.

THE FAMILY RUM PUNCH

SERVES 4 **PREP TIME** 5 MINUTES **TOTAL TIME** 5 MINUTES

2 cups apple juice, chilled

2 cups prepared lemonade, chilled

2 cups Tropicana fruit punch, chilled

2 cups club soda, chilled

12 ounces frozen mixed berries

4 ounces white rum

Ice

Mint leaves, for garnish

When I was growing up, there was a punch at every family event. Having a punch around meant fun! This can be made virgin, too (for the kids)!

Combine the apple juice, lemonade, fruit punch, club soda, berries, and rum in a pitcher. Serve in ice-filled glasses with mint leaves.

'BAMA SLAMMA

SERVES 4 **PREP TIME** 5 MINUTES **TOTAL TIME** 5 MINUTES

4 ounces Southern Comfort

4 ounces sloe gin

4 ounces amaretto

4 ounces fresh lime juice

8 ounces orange juice

Orange and lime peels, for garnish

This drink gets me twerking! It's bold yet refreshing. This one's not for the kids 🙊

Pour the Southern Comfort, gin, amaretto, lime juice, and orange juice into a cocktail shaker. Shake to combine. Pour into glasses and top with the orange and lime peels. Bottoms up!

POMEGRANATE-BASIL SPRITZER

SERVES 4 **PREP TIME** 5 MINUTES **TOTAL TIME** 10 MINUTES

2 cups pomegranate juice

2 cups club soda

1 cup pomegranate seeds

4 ounces sloe gin

8 lime slices

½ cup torn fresh basil leaves

4 tablespoons torn fresh mint leaves

Ice

If you're looking for a quick drink to pick you up gently and give you eagle's wings, this is the drink for you!

Combine the pomegranate juice, club soda, ½ cup of the pomegranate seeds, gin, lime slices, ¼ cup of the basil, and 2 tablespoons of the mint leaves in a pitcher and stir. Pour into four ice-filled glasses and garnish with the remaining pomegranate seeds, basil, and mint.

OLD-FASHIONED NYC CHOCOLATE MILK

SERVES 2 **TOTAL TIME** 5 MINUTES

⅔ cup Fox's U-Bet chocolate syrup

2 cups whole milk

1 cup seltzer

Whipped cream, for serving

Shaved chocolate, for serving

Marshmallows, for serving

Chocolate sprinkles, for serving

I am a big chocolate milk lover! I sometimes order it out at restaurants and diners, and the waiters definitely look at me funny, but IDC. This frothy, creamy chocolate milk is a chocolate milk lover's dream come true. The Fox's U-Bet chocolate syrup makes this drink a NYC classic.

Divide the chocolate syrup, milk, and seltzer between two cups. Stir until well combined. Top each cup with whipped cream, shaved chocolate, marshmallows, and sprinkles. Drink and make a mustache. ☺

FOOD IS AT THE CENTER OF HOW I DEFINE FAMILY, CULTURE, HERITAGE, AND THE FUTURE. EVERY RECIPE THAT HAS BEEN PASSED DOWN FROM MY GRANDMOTHER, TO MY FATHER, AND NOW TO ME IS ALIVE, FULL OF STORY, AND RICH IN ESSENCE. WHEN I COOK FOR OTHERS, I GET TO SHARE THIS LEGACY.

—*Lazarus Lynch*

SLAYIN' SOUPS AND STEWS

ROTISSERIE CHICKEN TACO SOUP

SERVES 6 **PREP TIME** 15 MINUTES **TOTAL TIME** 1 HOUR 10 MINUTES

1 red bell pepper

2 tablespoons olive oil

1 medium white onion, chopped

1 large jalapeño, seeded and chopped

2 small garlic cloves, chopped

1 tablespoon ancho chili powder

1 teaspoon ground cumin

1 teaspoon smoked paprika

Kosher salt and freshly ground black pepper

6 cups low-sodium chicken stock, plus more as needed

1 cup thawed frozen or cooked fresh corn kernels

One (15-ounce) can pinto beans, drained and rinsed

One (10-ounce) can diced tomatoes with green chiles

One (3- to 4-pound) rotisserie chicken, bones and skin removed, meat shredded

Zest and juice of 1 lime, plus lime wedges for serving

Handful crushed Tostitos Hint of Lime tortilla chips, for serving

Sour cream, for serving

Shredded white cheddar cheese, for serving

½ cup chopped fresh cilantro, for serving

Taco trucks have been on the come-up for a minute now. When you find a good one, it's like finding gold. Whenever I'm in LA, I try to hit up a taco truck for some bomb tacos *al pastor*. I'm also a fan of the store-bought rotisserie chicken! A good one is always so juicy and tender. I've married all the best parts of a taco in this soup: the crunchy shell, juicy meat (thank you, store-bought rotisserie chicken, though you can roast your own, of course), and loads of my favorite toppings. You're gonna be in taco heaven with this soup.

Place the bell pepper directly over an open medium-high flame. Char, turning occasionally, until the skin is black on all sides, about 5 minutes. Turn off the heat, transfer the pepper to a bowl, cover tightly with plastic wrap or a kitchen towel, and set aside for about 5 minutes. Run the pepper under cold water, rubbing off the charred skin. Dry on a paper towel and roughly chop.

Heat the olive oil in a large stockpot over medium-high heat. Add the bell pepper, onion, jalapeño, and garlic and cook, stirring often, until softened, about 2 minutes. Add the chile powder, cumin, paprika, ½ teaspoon salt, and ¼ teaspoon black pepper. Cook spices, stirring, until lightly toasted, 1 to 2 minutes. Add the stock, corn, pinto beans, and tomatoes with chiles, and bring to a boil. Reduce the heat to low and simmer until the soup thickens and the flavors meld, about 30 minutes. For a thinner soup, add more stock as desired. Add the chicken, lime zest, and lime juice. Cook until the chicken is heated through, about 5 minutes more. Adjust the seasoning with salt and black pepper to taste.

To serve, divide the soup among six bowls and top with sour cream, cheddar, jalapeños, cilantro, and tortilla chips, and lime wedges alongside.

THE GRAVY

Charring peppers over direct heat brings out the natural flavors of peppers while giving them a smoky quality. Do not fear burning the peppers; that's kinda the point. Your stove might get a little messy from all the burnt skin and smoke alarms may go off. Don't worry, it's all for good reasons.

BEER-BRAISED OXTAIL AND BUTTERBEAN STEW

SERVES 6 **PREP TIME** 10 MINUTES **TOTAL TIME** 6 HOURS

3 pounds beef oxtails

2 teaspoons seasoning salt (such as Lawry's)

1 teaspoon ground allspice

½ teaspoon freshly ground black pepper

3 tablespoons vegetable or canola oil

1 medium yellow onion, chopped (about 1 cup)

3 scallions, chopped, plus more for serving

1 Roma (plum) tomato, roughly chopped

3 garlic cloves, chopped

2 tablespoons tomato paste

2 tablespoons Worcestershire sauce

1 tablespoon browning sauce (see page 18)

One (12-ounce) bottle lager beer

Two (14.1-ounce) cans butterbeans, drained and rinsed

1 cup low-sodium chicken stock

2 or 3 sprigs fresh thyme

1 Scotch bonnet pepper

Kosher salt and freshly ground black pepper

Rice and Peas (page 167) or white rice, for serving

Oxtails make me so happy. It's hearty and rich, and yes, it's the tails of cow. It's one of the tougher cuts of meat, which is why it needs a longer cooking time. While my dad is Southern and my mom is Guyanese, I swear I've got some Jamaican running up and down my veins. This stew takes me back to my childhood, when I would visit New Jerusalem, a Jamaican church, on a Sunday afternoon for lunch and have their oxtail dinners. The beer gives this stew a richer and more robust flavor. My oxtails are *gravy* with my Rice and Peas (page 167).

In a large bowl, season the oxtails with the seasoning salt, allspice, and black pepper.

Heat the oil in a large heavy-bottomed pot or Dutch oven over medium-high heat until almost smoking. Add the oxtails, working in batches, and cook, turning occasionally, until dark brown on all sides, about 10 minutes total. Transfer the oxtails to a plate.

In the same pot, cook the onion, scallions, tomato, and garlic over medium heat until softened, about 3 minutes. Stir in the tomato paste and cook for another minute. Add the Worcestershire and browning sauce and cook, stirring occasionally, for another minute. Return the oxtails to the pot and add the beer, butterbeans, stock, and thyme. Bring to a boil. Cover, reduce the heat to low, and cook for 5½ hours, until oxtails are falling off the bones. Uncover the pot, add the Scotch bonnet, and cook for 30 minutes more. Remove the Scotch bonnet and adjust seasoning with salt and black pepper to taste. Serve the stew hot over rice and peas or plain white rice. Garnish with scallions.

SLOW COOKER BLACK-EYED PEA <u>AND</u> SAUSAGE CHILI

SERVES 6 TO 8 **PREP TIME** 10 MINUTES **TOTAL TIME** 6 HOURS

1 pound frozen black-eyed peas, sorted and rinsed

4 hot Italian sausage links (about ½ pound), casings removed and meat separated

1 yellow onion, chopped (about 1½ cups)

2 celery stalks, chopped (about 1⅓ cups)

3 cups low-sodium chicken stock

2 garlic cloves, minced

2 teaspoons smoked paprika

2 teaspoons chili powder

1 teaspoon kosher salt

½ teaspoon freshly ground black pepper

½ teaspoon crushed red pepper flakes

2 tablespoons chopped fresh flat-leaf parsley, for serving

Black-eyed peas are the peas of the South, and my love for them runs deep. The Southern legend is that if you want to see more mullahs in the bank, eat lots of black-eyed peas and collard greens on New Year's Day. (I did say it was a legend.) This chili is a lot like Hoppin' John in that it's comforting and robust yet basic AF. The sausage adds a depth of smokiness and spice to this dish. I love eating this chili over Carolina Gold white rice or simply by itself. This recipe is a new addition to the family archives; it's got soul, and it ain't fancy.

In a slow cooker, combine the black-eyed peas, sausage, onion, celery, stock, garlic, paprika, chili powder, salt, black pepper, and red pepper flakes. Cover and cook on High until the beans are tender and the stew has thickened, about 6 hours. Season to taste with more salt and black pepper.

Serve topped with the parsley.

THE GRAVY

If using dried black-eyed peas, cover peas in a pot with 4 inches of cold water and soak overnight. Drain and rinse the peas the next day. Alternatively, use the quick-soaking method: Cover peas in cold water and bring to a boil for 2 minutes, remove from heat, cover the pot with a lid, and let peas stand for 1 hour. Drain and rinse peas.

MOM'S SPLIT PEA AND HAM SOUP WITH GREEN PLANTAIN CHIPS

SERVES 6 **PREP TIME** 10 MINUTES **TOTAL TIME** 1 HOUR 30 MINUTES

SOUP

1 tablespoon extra-virgin olive oil

1 medium yellow onion, chopped

2 medium carrots, chopped

1 celery stalk, chopped

1 medium red bell pepper, seeded and chopped

2 garlic cloves, smashed

Kosher salt and freshly ground black pepper

1 ham bone with meat

1 pound dried green split peas, sorted and rinsed

8 cups low-sodium chicken or vegetable stock

2 teaspoons fresh thyme leaves (about 6 sprigs)

2 green plantains, peeled and chopped

Fresh flat-leaf parsley, for serving

PLANTAIN CHIPS

Canola oil, for frying

1 green plantain, peeled and slized into ⅛-inch-thick rounds

Kosher salt

We have a little tradition in my family after Thanksgiving: We save the ham bone to make this split pea soup the next day. I've dubbed this my mom's recipe because it's got her name written all over it. She remembers making this soup only a handful of times, but I remember eating it year after year. These days, I garnish the soup with fried plantain chips to bring in some crunch. This soup is the most comforting thing to me. And it's Mom-approved!

Make the soup: In a 4-quart stockpot over medium heat, heat the oil and sauté the onion, carrots, celery, bell pepper, garlic, 1 teaspoon salt, and ½ teaspoon pepper, until softened, stirring occasionally, 10 to 15 minutes. Transfer the vegetables to a bowl and set aside.

Meanwhile, slice the remaining meat off the ham bone and set the meat aside in a clean bowl. Place the ham bone, split peas, chicken stock, thyme, and 1 teaspoon salt into the stockpot, and bring to a full boil over medium-high heat. Boil for 2 minutes. Shut off the heat, cover the pot, and let stand for 1 hour.

After 1 hour, return the sautéed vegetables to the pot and bring everything to a boil over medium heat for 1 hour and 10 minutes. Add the plantains, reduce the heat to medium-low, and cook until the peas and plantains are softened, about 20 minutes more. The peas should pretty much dissolve in the soup. Season the soup with more salt and black pepper.

Make the plantain chips: Heat 2 inches of canola oil in a large skillet or medium saucepan over medium-high heat to a temperature of 360°F. Add the plantains to the hot oil in small batches and cook, turning occasionally, until crisp and light golden brown, about 2 minutes. Using a slotted spoon or spider, transfer the plantain chips to a paper towel–lined plate to drain. Hit the chips with some salt.

To serve, divide the soup among six bowls and top with some of the reserved ham meat, plantain chips, and parsley.

THE GRAVY

To peel plantains, use a sharp knife to slice both ends of the plantain. Using the tip of the knife, make a slit lengthwise through the outer green skin, being careful not to slice through the flesh of the plantain, and peel.

THE GRAVY

I like to make this soup, minus the Parmesan, toward the end of the summer, right when tomato season is ending, and freeze it for up to 3 months in an airtight container. To reheat, place the frozen soup into a pot with 1 cup of water or stock, cover, and thaw over medium heat until soup is hot and reaches an internal temperature of 165°F (use a thermometer). Stir in the Parmesan and more fresh basil before serving.

CHUNKY TOMATO SOUP WITH MAD PARMESAN

SERVES 6 **PREP TIME** 10 MINUTES **TOTAL TIME** 1 HOUR 20 MINUTES

3 pounds ripe Roma (plum) or other tomatoes, halved

¼ cup plus 2 tablespoons extra-virgin olive oil

Kosher salt

½ teaspoon crushed red pepper flakes, plus more to taste

2 cups small-diced Spanish onions

6 garlic cloves, minced

3 cups low-sodium chicken stock

5 sprigs fresh thyme

½ cup freshly grated Parmesan cheese, plus more for serving

½ cup fresh basil leaves, plus more for garnish

Tomato soup and grilled cheese—I'm a fan of the combo! It's nostalgic and brilliant. The South is abundant with tomatoes, and they taste best when they are in season during the summer. That's also the best time to make this soup. I start out by roasting my tomatoes and garlic until the tomatoes burst and the garlic starts to soften and sweeten. Then I puree them and serve the soup with maddddddd Parmesan! This soup also tastes great the next day, but it doesn't usually last more than 24 hours for me. It goes great with my Pimiento Spread and Tomato Grilled Cheese (page 123).

Preheat the oven to 450°F. Line a baking sheet with two sheets of aluminum foil.

In a medium bowl, toss the tomatoes with ¼ cup of the olive oil, 1 teaspoon salt, and the red pepper flakes. Arrange the tomatoes cut-side up on the aluminum foil. Roast for 35 to 40 minutes, until the tomatoes are bursting and lightly browned.

Heat the remaining 2 tablespoons oil in a large Dutch oven or heavy-bottomed pot over medium-high heat. Add the onions and cook, stirring occasionally, until softened, 5 to 6 minutes. Season lightly with salt. Stir in the garlic and cook until fragrant, about 2 minutes more. Add the roasted tomatoes (and all the juices from the baking sheet) and break them up with a wooden spoon. Add the stock and thyme and bring to a boil. Reduce the heat to low and simmer for 25 to 30 minutes. Turn off the heat and remove the thyme. Stir in the Parmesan and basil. (For a smoother soup, use a blender and blend until you reach the desired consistency.)

Ladle the soup into six bowls and season with salt and red pepper flakes to taste. Serve with extra Parmesan and basil on top.

SKILLET TURKEY CHILI WITH CHEESY JALAPEÑO CORNBREAD CRUST

SERVES 8 TO 10 **PREP TIME** 10 MINUTES **TOTAL TIME** 1 HOUR 25 MINUTES

TURKEY CHILI

1 tablespoon olive oil

1 small white onion, chopped (about 1 cup)

½ teaspoon kosher salt

1 small bell pepper (any color), chopped

1 garlic clove, minced

1 pound ground turkey

2 teaspoons chili powder

1 teaspoon smoked paprika

½ teaspoon ground cumin

¼ teaspoon cayenne pepper

¼ teaspoon ground cinnamon

1 tablespoon tomato paste

¼ teaspoon freshly ground black pepper, plus more to taste

One (28-ounce) can fire-roasted tomatoes with chopped green chiles

One (15.5-ounce) can black beans

One (15.5-ounce) can red kidney beans

1 jalapeño, seeded and diced

I've become, especially in the winter, a chili-and-cornbread head lately. I make this recipe all the time, and it always hits the spot. Chili can be as complex or as simple as you want it to be. I make a vegetarian one with cauliflower, mushrooms, and poblano (page 104) that's bonkers! Here, I actually use the same nonsweet cornbread recipe on page 179 and cut all the amounts in half. This is great for breakfast too the next day with a fried egg on top!!

Make the chili: Heat the oil in a 12-inch cast-iron skillet over medium-high heat. Add the onion and ¼ teaspoon of the salt and cook, stirring occasionally, until translucent, 1 to 2 minutes. Add the bell pepper and garlic and cook until the pepper is soft, about 3 minutes.

Add the ground turkey, chili powder, paprika, cumin, cayenne, and cinnamon. Cook, breaking up the meat with a wooden spoon or spatula as it cooks, until the meat is browned, 6 to 8 minutes. Stir in the tomato paste and cook for another minute, stirring occasionally. Add the tomatoes, black beans, kidney beans, and jalapeño. Bring the chili to a boil, then reduce the heat to low and simmer until the chili thickens, about 20 minutes. Add ¼ cup water if the chili gets thicker than your liking. Season with the remaining ¼ teaspoon salt and black pepper.

CORNBREAD TOPPING

½ cup stone-ground cornmeal

½ cup all-purpose flour

1 teaspoon sugar

¾ teaspoon baking powder

¼ teaspoon baking soda

¼ teaspoon kosher salt

½ cup buttermilk

6 tablespoons (¾ stick) unsalted butter, melted

1 large egg, lightly beaten

Kernels from 1 ear corn

1 small jalapeño, seeded and chopped

½ cup shredded cheddar or Jack cheese

2 tablespoons chopped fresh cilantro, for serving

Make the cornbread topping: Preheat the oven to 425°F.

In a large bowl, whisk together the cornmeal, flour, sugar, baking powder, baking soda, and salt. Whisk in the buttermilk, melted butter, and egg until smooth. Stir in the corn and jalapeño.

Pour the mixture over the chili and spread it evenly with a spatula. Sprinkle with the cheese and bake until the top is golden brown and the cheese has melted, 20 to 25 minutes.

Sprinkle with the cilantro and let rest for 10 minutes before serving.

VEGGIE CHILI PIZZA

SERVES 8 TO 10 **PREP TIME** 10 MINUTES **TOTAL TIME** 1 HOUR

1 small head cauliflower, cut into small florets

2 cups chopped portobello mushrooms

1 poblano pepper, steamed, seeded and chopped

2 teaspoons smoked Spanish paprika

2 teaspoons chipotle chili powder

1 garlic clove, finely minced

¼ teaspoon kosher salt

¼ teaspoon ground cinnamon

¼ teaspoon ground coriander

¼ teaspoon ground cumin

Large pinch crushed red pepper flakes

1 tablespoon olive oil

One (15-ounce) can black beans, drained

One (10-ounce) can fire-roasted diced tomatoes and green chiles

2 cups low-sodium vegetable broth

Splash of your favorite hot sauce

I'm a New Yorker and I love NYC-style pizza. The thinner, the crisper, the more burnt bubbles of cheese, the better. I sometimes cheat on my NYC-style pizza with my veggie chili pizza. The crust is a slammin' cornbread, the veggies are charred until borderline burnt in the best way, and the whole thing gets glowed up with all the finest bling bling: cheddar, jalapeños, and sour cream! Once you taste this chili pizza goodness, you will understand my obsession.

Make the chili: Preheat the oven to 500°F.

On a rimmed baking sheet, toss together the cauliflower, mushrooms, poblano, paprika, chipotle chili powder, salt, cinnamon, coriander, cumin, red pepper flakes, and olive oil. Arrange the vegetables in a single layer and roast until browned and tender, 10 to 12 minutes. Reduce the oven temperature to 425°F.

Carefully transfer the vegetables to a large pot (set the baking sheet aside) and stir in the garlic, beans, tomatoes with green chiles, broth, and hot sauce. Bring the mixture to a boil over medium-high heat, stirring occasionally, then reduce the heat to medium-low and simmer until the chili reaches your desired thickness, about 20 minutes total. Add more broth or water for a looser chili.

Meanwhile, make the crust: Grease the same baking sheet pan you cooked the vegetables on with the oil.

In a large bowl, whisk together the cornmeal, flour, sugar, baking powder, baking soda, and salt. Whisk in the eggs, buttermilk, and melted butter until combined.

CORNBREAD CRUST

1 tablespoon olive oil

1 cup stone-ground yellow cornmeal

¾ cup all-purpose flour

2 teaspoons sugar

¼ teaspoon baking powder

½ teaspoon baking soda

½ teaspoon kosher salt

2 large eggs, lightly beaten

¾ cup buttermilk

6 tablespoons (¾ stick) unsalted butter, melted and cooled

TOPPING

¾ cup grated sharp cheddar cheese

Sliced jalapeños

Sour cream

Fresh cilantro

Pour the batter onto the prepared baking sheet and spread to the edges. Top with the chili and cheddar, leaving a ½-inch border. Bake until the cornbread is done and the cheese has melted, 15 to 17 minutes.

Remove from the oven and let cool slightly before serving.

Top with jalapeños, sour cream, and cilantro as desired; slice; and serve.

NEVER DIM YOUR LIGHT FOR

FEAR OF BEING TOO BRIGHT.

LET YOUR LIGHT SHINE!

LIGHT CARRIES TRANSFORMING
ENERGY.

LET IT SHINE!

—*Lazarus Lynch*

LIT BURGERS AND 'WICHES

SPICY BUTTERMILK FRIED CHICKEN SANDWICH

SERVES 4   **PREP TIME** 20 MINUTES   **TOTAL TIME** 50 MINUTES

FRIED CHICKEN

4 boneless, skinless or skin-on chicken thighs

1 cup buttermilk

2 large eggs

¼ cup your favorite hot sauce

3 tablespoons House Seasoning Blend (recipe follows)

½ teaspoon cayenne pepper

2 cups all-purpose flour

⅓ cup cornstarch

1 teaspoon baking powder

Canola oil, for frying

SPREAD

1 cup mayonnaise

1 tablespoon Dijon mustard

1 teaspoon fresh lemon juice

½ teaspoon celery seeds

Splash of pickle brine (from a jar of pickles)

Splash of hot sauce

¼ teaspoon freshly ground black pepper

Is there anything bad to say about fried chicken? Nah. I first made this recipe on the *Today* show. One of the anchors, Sheinelle Jones, said it was the best fried chicken she'd ever had, and she wasn't lying, y'all. I thought I was over the fried chicken sandwich hype until I saw how people were taking to this sandwich on social media. People were tweeting me pics of their fried chicken, and families were completely switching dinner plans to make this recipe instead of going out—that's when I knew I'd hit a nerve. Watch out, Shake Shack, haha!

Make the fried chicken: Place the chicken thighs in a shallow container.

In a medium bowl, whisk together the buttermilk, eggs, hot sauce, 2 tablespoons House Seasoning, and the cayenne. Pour the buttermilk mixture over the chicken and turn the pieces to coat evenly. Cover the container with a lid or plastic wrap. Refrigerate for at least 30 minutes and up to 24 hours.

When ready to cook the chicken, preheat the oven to 350°F. Line a baking sheet with aluminum foil and set a wire rack on top.

Remove the chicken from the refrigerator.

In a medium bowl, whisk together the flour, cornstarch, remaining 1 tablespoon House Seasoning, and the baking powder. Add 2 tablespoons of the buttermilk marinade (what the chicken was soaking in) to the flour mixture and use a fork to mix gently to create small clumps. This will add texture to the fried chicken.

Fill a cast-iron skillet or heavy-bottomed pot with oil to a depth of 2 inches and heat over medium-high heat to 350°F.

RECIPE AND INGREDIENTS CONTINUE >>>

ASSEMBLY

4 potato rolls (I like Martin's), lightly toasted

Sliced iceberg lettuce

Sliced heirloom tomatoes

Bread and butter pickles

Your favorite hot sauce

Dredge the chicken pieces in the flour mixture on all sides. Shake off any excess flour. Working in batches to avoid crowding the pot, add the chicken to the hot oil and fry until golden brown and crisp on both sides, 4 to 5 minutes per side. Once all the chicken is cooked, transfer the prepared baking sheet to the oven. Bake until a meat thermometer inserted into the chicken registers 165°F, about 10 minutes more.

Make the spread: In a small bowl, mix together the mayonnaise, mustard, lemon juice, celery seeds, pickle brine, hot sauce, and black pepper.

Assemble the sandwiches: Spread some of the seasoned mayonnaise on both sides of the rolls.

Pile the bottoms of the rolls with lettuce, tomato, fried chicken, pickles, and loads of hot sauce, then add the top bun.

HOUSE SEASONING

MAKES ½ CUP   TOTAL TIME: 1 MINUTE

2 tablespoons sweet paprika	1 tablespoon dried oregano
1 tablespoon cayenne pepper	1 tablespoon kosher salt
1 tablespoon onion powder	1 tablespoon freshly ground black pepper
1 tablespoon garlic powder	

In a small bowl, combine the paprika, cayenne, onion powder, garlic powder, oregano, salt, and pepper. Use immediately or store in an airtight container or mason jar in a cool, dry place for up to 1 month.

THE GRAVY

If you can't handle the heat (like some spice Daredevils), take out the cayenne pepper and use 1 tablespoon hot sauce. You really shouldn't skip on the hot sauce for that extra flavor.

BLACKENED SALMON BURGER WITH CUCUMBER SAUCE

SERVES 4   **PREP TIME** 15 MINUTES   **TOTAL TIME** 40 MINUTES

BLACKENED SEASONING MIX

1 tablespoon smoked paprika

2 teaspoons kosher salt

2 teaspoons freshly ground black pepper

2 teaspoons onion powder

2 teaspoons garlic powder

2 teaspoons coarsely chopped fresh thyme leaves

½ teaspoon cayenne pepper

CUCUMBER SAUCE

½ cup full-fat or 2% Greek yogurt

⅓ small cucumber, diced (about ⅓ cup)

Juice of 1 lemon

2 teaspoons chopped fresh dill

SALMON PATTIES

1 pound skinless, boneless salmon fillet, cut into 1-inch cubes

2 tablespoons plus 1 teaspoon canola oil

If you put me on a tropical island and gave me a grill on the sand, these are the burgers I would make. I never made salmon burgers until writing this book. I felt like most burgers erred on the heavier and meatier side, and I wanted to make a burger that was equal in its flavor command, but lighter on the tummy. These burgers are just what I imagined, and they are now my gift to you.

Make the seasoning mix: In a small bowl, combine the paprika, salt, black pepper, onion powder, garlic powder, thyme, and cayenne. Set aside.

Make the cucumber sauce: In a food processor, mix together the yogurt, cucumber, lemon juice, and dill until chunky. Transfer to a bowl and set aside.

Make the salmon patties: Place a piece of parchment paper on a cutting board.

In the bowl of a food processor, pulse together the salmon and 2 tablespoons of the oil until it resembles coarsely ground meat.

Using a spatula, transfer the salmon to the parchment paper and divide it into 4 equal balls. Press down on each ball to form a patty. Generously season one side of each patty with 1 teaspoon of the seasoning blend. Wash your hands.

Assemble the burgers: Heat a flat-top griddle or cast-iron skillet over medium-high heat.

Spread the butter on the inside of the potato rolls and toast on the griddle. Transfer to a plate.

ASSEMBLY

2 tablespoons unsalted butter, at room temperature

4 potato rolls (I like Martin's)

Soft tender microgreens, for serving

1 avocado, pitted, peeled, and sliced, for serving

Wipe any excess butter off the griddle with a paper towel. Heat the remaining 1 teaspoon oil on the griddle over medium-high heat. Add the salmon patties, seasoned-side down, and sprinkle the other side with more seasoning blend. Cook until dark brown, about 3 minutes. Flip the patties and reduce the heat to medium. Cook until golden brown on the second side, 2 to 3 minutes more. Remove from the heat.

Top the toasted bottom buns with a few pieces of lettuce. Place the patties on top of the lettuce, then add the cucumber sauce and sliced avocado. Add the top bun and serve.

BLACK-EYED PEA BURGER WITH SPICY CABBAGE SLAW

MAKES 4 BURGERS **PREP TIME** 15 MINUTES **TOTAL TIME** 25 MINUTES

SPICY CABBAGE SLAW

1 cup thinly sliced cabbage

1 Gala apple, cored and sliced into ¼-inch-thick matchsticks

1 tablespoon Sriracha

Juice of 1 lemon

BURGERS

One (15.5-ounce) can black-eyed peas, drained, rinsed, and mashed with a fork

½ cup chopped red bell pepper

¼ cup grated onion

1 garlic clove, grated

1½ teaspoons chili powder

½ teaspoon dried oregano

¼ cup plain Italian breadcrumbs

1 large egg, beaten

¼ teaspoon kosher salt

¼ teaspoon freshly ground black pepper

Dash of hot sauce

1 tablespoon canola oil

4 potato rolls, lightly toasted, for serving

This burger is 100 percent vegetarian and 100 percent to-die-for. If you've ever got leftover black-eyed peas, mash them and turn them into some patties.

Make the spicy cabbage slaw: In a large bowl, toss together the cabbage, apple, Sriracha, and lemon juice. Set aside.

Make the burgers: In a large bowl, mix together the black-eyed peas, bell pepper, onion, garlic, chili powder, and oregano. Add the breadcrumbs, egg, salt, black pepper, and hot sauce. Mix until well combined. Form the black-eyed pea mixture into 4 equal patties.

Heat the oil in a large skillet over medium-high heat. Add the patties and cook until golden brown on both sides, about 2 minutes per side.

Transfer the patties to the bottom buns and top with the slaw and top bun.

CRAB CAKES
WITH CHIPOTLE RÉMOULADE

MAKES 8 CRAB CAKES **PREP TIME** 15 MINUTES **TOTAL TIME** 45 MINUTES

CHIPOTLE RÉMOULADE

½ cup mayonnaise

1 small shallot, roughly chopped

1 garlic clove, smashed

1 tablespoon adobo sauce (from a can of chipotle peppers in adobo)

2 teaspoons fresh lemon juice

1¼ teaspoons Old Bay seasoning, divided

CRAB CAKES

¼ cup mayonnaise

2 large egg yolks

1 tablespoon chopped fresh dill

1 tablespoon Dijon mustard

1 pound jumbo lump crabmeat

1¼ cups panko breadcrumbs

2 tablespoons canola oil, plus more as needed

1 tablespoon unsalted butter, plus more as needed

8 brioche rolls or slider buns, lightly toasted

2 cups baby arugula

There are a few things I think everyone should know how to make really well: scrambled eggs, roast chicken (hey, Ina Garten), and crab cakes. Why crab cakes? First, because I love them, and second, because I love them. A good crab cake is all about the crab. I normally like to serve my crab cakes with a squeeze of lemon, or, on other occasions, with a bangin' sauce, aka chipotle rémoulade. Even though these crab cakes aren't technically a sandwich, I felt like breaking rules and strongly recommending you to eat these cakes between two pieces of carbs! This recipe is nothing to be intimidated about, and it will seriously impress.

Make the chipotle mayo: In a food processor, blend the mayonnaise, shallot, garlic, adobo sauce, lemon juice, and ¼ teaspoon Old Bay seasoning. Transfer to a bowl, cover, and refrigerate until ready to use.

Make the crab cakes: In a large bowl, mix together the mayonnaise, egg yolks, dill, and mustard. Add the crabmeat, ¾ cup of the breadcrumbs, and the remaining 1 teaspoon Old Bay and stir to combine. Let stand in refrigerator for 10 minutes.

Line a baking sheet with parchment paper.

Fill a shallow dish with the remaining ½ cup breadcrumbs. Form the crab mixture into ¼-cup patties. Coat both sides of the crab cakes in the breadcrumbs, then place on the prepared baking sheet.

Heat the oil and butter in a large cast-iron skillet over medium-high heat. Working in batches so as not to overcrowd the pan, cook the crab cakes until golden brown on each side, 2 to 3 minutes per side. Transfer to a paper towel–lined plate. Repeat to cook the remaining crab cakes, adding more oil and butter to the pan as needed between batches.

Spread rémoulade on buns, and place a crab cake on each bottom half. Top the crab cakes with arugula and serve immediately.

SHORTY'S SHORT RIB SLIDERS WITH DAD'S CREAMY COLESLAW <u>AND</u> HOUSE PICKLES

SERVES 8 **PREP TIME** 10 MINUTES **TOTAL TIME** 3 HOURS 55 MINUTES

SHORT RIBS

3½ to 4 pounds short ribs

1 tablespoon smoked paprika

2 teaspoons kosher salt

½ teaspoon freshly ground black pepper

BOURBON BARBECUE SAUCE

1 cup ketchup

½ cup bourbon

3 tablespoons packed light brown sugar

2 tablespoons Worcestershire sauce

1 tablespoon apple cider vinegar

1 tablespoon yellow mustard

1 teaspoon onion powder

1 teaspoon chili powder

1 garlic clove, minced

½ teaspoon crushed red pepper flakes

ASSEMBLY

8 slider rolls, lightly toasted

Dad's Creamy Coleslaw (page 152), for serving

I get excited at the thought of ribs being brined, cured, or seasoned in marinade for hours, then slowly smoked, or roasted, or 'cued 'til their juices perfume my kitchen (or wherever I may be). This is how the pit masters and barbecue magicians, whom I undoubtedly respect, throw down. I am not even close to a pit master, but these shorty's short rib sliders were approved by my very opinionated family. The bourbon barbecue sauce makes me want to break dance. I make the coleslaw a day before so the flavors get to meld and the cabbage wilts. If you don't make your own pickles, you can use bread and butter pickles from the store. (I won't judge you.)

Make the ribs: Preheat the oven to 300°F.

Place the ribs in a roasting pan. Sprinkle all sides of the short ribs with paprika, salt, and black pepper.

Pour ½ cup cold water into the roasting pan. Cover the pan with aluminum foil and bake the short ribs until very tender, about 3 hours. Increase the oven temperature to 400°F and remove the foil. Roast until ribs are golden brown and slightly crispy around the edges, about 30 minutes. Transfer the ribs and their juices to a bowl. Using two forks, shred the meat and discard the bones.

While the ribs cook, make the bourbon barbecue sauce: In a small saucepan, mix together the ketchup, bourbon, brown sugar, Worcestershire, vinegar, yellow mustard, onion powder, chili powder, garlic, and red pepper flakes. Bring to a boil over medium-high heat, then reduce the heat to low and cook the barbecue sauce until thickened, about 15 minutes.

Assemble the sliders: Pour the sauce over the meat and toss together. Divide the meat evenly among the slider buns and top with coleslaw.

THE HOT CATFISH SANDWICH WITH RANCH SAUCE

SERVES 4 **PREP TIME** 20 MINUTES **TOTAL TIME** 45 MINUTES

RANCH SAUCE

½ cup mayonnaise

¼ cup sour cream

¼ cup buttermilk

2 tablespoons chopped fresh flat-leaf parsley or chives, or a mix

1 garlic clove, grated

1 teaspoon hot sauce

CATFISH

Four (4- to 6-ounce) catfish fillets

1 lemon

Kosher salt and freshly ground black pepper

2 cups canola oil, for frying

¾ cup buttermilk

1 large egg

2 tablespoons your favorite vinegar-based hot sauce (I like Frank's RedHot)

4 teaspoons Old Bay seasoning

1 cup self-rising flour

¼ cup stone-ground yellow cornmeal

2 teaspoons cayenne pepper

1 teaspoon packed dark brown sugar

I've grown to love catfish from the days of my dad's restaurant. He sold mostly whiting and porgy fish, but every now and again, customers would order fried catfish on wheat or white bread with some hot sauce on top. I prepare this recipe like Nashville's Hot Chicken. Whenever I'm in Nashville, Tennessee, I find time to get my hands on some hot chicken! This sandwich combines my love for my dad's fried catfish and for Nashville's hot chicken. Also, the ranch sauce is chronic. Beware.

Make the ranch sauce: In a medium bowl, whisk together the mayonnaise, sour cream, buttermilk, parsley, garlic, and hot sauce until smooth. Cover and refrigerate until ready to use, up to 1 week.

Make the catfish: Place the catfish on a tray and squeeze the lemon over it. Season both sides with 1 teaspoon salt and ½ teaspoon black pepper.

Heat the canola oil in a cast-iron skillet over medium-high heat until the oil reaches 360°F. Line a baking sheet with aluminum foil and set a wire rack on top.

In a large bowl, whisk together the buttermilk, egg, hot sauce, and 2 teaspoons of the Old Bay.

In a shallow dish, whisk together the flour, cornmeal, 1 teaspoon of the Old Bay, and 1 teaspoon black pepper. Dip the fish in the buttermilk mixture, then coat in the flour. Shake off any excess flour and dip in the buttermilk mixture again, then finally the flour, shaking off any excess.

RECIPE AND INGREDIENTS CONTINUE »

HOUSE PICKLES
(page 78)

1 teaspoon sweet paprika

1 teaspoon chili powder

½ teaspoon garlic powder

ASSEMBLY

4 slices thick-cut white bread

House Pickles (page 78),
  for serving

Old Bay Potato Chips
  (page 71), for serving

Add the catfish pieces to the hot oil and fry until crisp and golden brown on the first side, about 3 minutes. Flip and fry until the catfish is cooked through and the second side is crisp and golden brown, about 3 minutes more. Drain on the prepared baking sheet. Continue frying all pieces, using more oil when necessary. Leave the frying oil in the pot, but turn off the heat and let the oil cool slightly.

In a heatproof bowl, whisk together the cayenne pepper, brown sugar, paprika, chili powder, garlic powder, remaining 1 teaspoon Old Bay, and ¼ cup of the hot oil from the skillet. Brush the seasoned oil sauce over both sides of the catfish.

Serve the hot catfish on white bread and drizzle with the ranch sauce spilling over the top. Serve with House Pickles and Old Bay Potato Chips.

PIMIENTO SPREAD AND TOMATO GRILLED CHEESE

SERVES 4   **PREP TIME** 10 MINUTES   **TOTAL TIME** 25 MINUTES

PIMIENTO CHEESE SPREAD

One (4-ounce) jar chopped pimientos, drained

4 ounces cheddar cheese, shredded

4 ounces cream cheese, at room temperature

1 tablespoon mayonnaise

1 teaspoon yellow mustard

½ teaspoon dried red chili flakes

½ teaspoon freshly ground black pepper

SANDWICH

¼ cup mayonnaise

8 pieces country white bread

4 slices vine-ripened tomato

4 slices sharp cheddar cheese (about 2 ounces)

4 slices pepper Jack cheese (about 2 ounces)

I've fallen so deeply in love with this pimiento cheese spread that I want to put it on literally everything. My sandwich pet peeve is a sandwich without even distribution of ingredients. So please spread everything wall-to-wall, love up those corners with spread—don't go cheap on me, people. For a nice golden crust, cook this sandwich in a hot cast-iron skillet and spread mayo on the bread (yep—I said mayonnaise) instead of butter. This sandwich pairs well with my CHUNKY Tomato Soup with MAD Parmesan (page 101), and is great for a weekend brunch.

Make the pimiento cheese spread: Pat the pimientos dry with a paper towel and put them in a medium bowl. Add the cheddar, cream cheese, mayonnaise, mustard, red chili flakes, and black pepper and mix until smooth and spreadable, about 2 minutes. Cover and refrigerate until ready to use, up to 1 week.

Heat a flat-top griddle or skillet over medium heat.

Spread the mayo over one side of each slice of bread. Place the bread mayo-side down on a clean work surface. Spread 1 tablespoon of the pimiento cheese on 4 slices of the bread. Top the other 4 slices with 1 slice each of the tomato, cheddar, and pepper Jack. Close the sandwiches and place them on the griddle. Cook until golden brown on one side, about 2 minutes. Flip and cook until the cheese has melted, 2 to 3 minutes more.

Slice the sandwiches in half diagonally and serve.

STICKY PORK BURGERS WITH HOT-AND-SOUR CABBAGE

SERVES 4 **PREP TIME** 15 MINUTES **TOTAL TIME** 55 MINUTES

MAYO SPREAD

½ cup mayonnaise

2 tablespoons Sriracha

HOT-AND-SOUR CABBAGE

2 cups shredded napa cabbage

¼ cup unseasoned rice vinegar

2 teaspoons grated fresh ginger

2 teaspoons sugar

½ teaspoon kosher salt

¼ teaspoon crushed red pepper flakes

PORK BURGERS

½ cup shredded napa cabbage

4 tablespoons olive oil

1 tablespoon grated fresh ginger

2 scallions, roughly chopped

1 small shallot, roughly chopped

2 garlic cloves, minced (1 tablespoon)

1 pound 80% lean ground pork

1 tablespoon low-sodium soy sauce

I lived in Beijing, China, for three months the summer of 2013. I was a junior in high school and didn't speak a lick of Mandarin. It wasn't long before I became obsessed with Chinese food and culture, and have been trying to transport my taste buds back ever since; this burger does just that. I make them with ground pork, because the pig can handle all the bold Asian flavors. Side note: I'm drooling just thinking about the layers of this burger: seasoned mayo, a umami-flavored juicy patty, and soft bread. The hot-and-sour cabbage is low-key like kimchi (not Chinese at all), but works here to break up the sweet and savory elements of the burger. I'm a big fan of sticky sauces lacquered on my meats and burgers. I lather these pork burgers in honey, then coat them in sesame seeds. This burger beautifully captures my love for bold Chinese flavors.

Make the mayo spread: In a small bowl, whisk together the mayonnaise and Sriracha. Cover and refrigerate until ready to use.

Make the hot-and-sour cabbage: Place the cabbage in a large bowl and set aside.

In a small saucepan, combine the vinegar, ginger, sugar, salt, and red pepper flakes and bring to a boil over medium-high heat, stirring, until the sugar has dissolved, 1 to 2 minutes. Shut off the heat and pour the vinegar mixture over the cabbage in the bowl. Toss to combine and set aside, tossing occasionally.

Make the pork burgers: In the bowl of a food processor, pulse together the ½ cup shredded cabbage, 2 tablespoons of the olive oil, the ginger, scallions, shallot, and garlic until finely minced. Transfer the cabbage mixture to a large bowl.

2 teaspoons untoasted sesame oil

½ teaspoon salt

¼ teaspoon red pepper flakes

¼ cup sesame seeds

¼ cup honey

4 seeded buns, split and lightly toasted

Add the pork, soy sauce, sesame oil, salt, and red pepper flakes to the bowl and mix well. Divide the pork mixture into 4 equal balls and form them into 1-inch-thick patties.

Place the sesame seeds in a shallow dish.

Heat the remaining 2 tablespoons olive oil in a large cast-iron skillet over medium-high heat. Add the burgers and cook until golden brown on the bottom, about 5 minutes. Flip and cook until cooked through, about 4 minutes more. Reduce the heat to low and pour the honey over the burgers, coating the tops and bottoms. Using a pair of tongs, remove the burgers from the skillet and roll them in the sesame seeds.

Spread the mayo spread on the toasted buns and place a sticky pork burger on each bottom bun. Top with some of the cabbage slaw and the top bun and serve.

DAD'S FRIED FISH SANDWICHES WITH TARTAR SAUCE

SERVES 5 **PREP TIME** 5 MINUTES **TOTAL TIME** 20 MINUTES

Canola oil, for deep-frying

3 cups self-rising flour, such as Aunt Jemima

3 tablespoons seafood seasoning, such as Old Bay

1 lemon, halved

10 pieces whiting fillet fish

1 cup mayonnaise

¼ cup sweet pickle relish

1 tablespoon pickle relish juice (from a jar of relish)

10 slices whole wheat or white bread

There's so much history attached to this recipe. Fried fish is a cultural experience in the black community. Folks fry fish for everything: church fund-raisers, block parties, and in their homes to feed the neighbors. Pops dropped orders of fish sandwiches at the restaurant on the reg, and they would sell out in a flash. People thought he used a secret seasoning blend, but it was just seafood seasoning and Aunt Jemima self-rising flour (the secret's out). Each sandwich came with one tartar sauce, but people would always request an extra because it was so good. There is not a single dish that represents the days of Dad's restaurant more than this one.

Fill a Dutch oven or heavy-bottomed pot with oil to a depth of 3 inches and heat over medium-high heat to 365°F.

In a shallow dish, combine the flour and seafood seasoning.

Squeeze the lemon over the fish and dredge the fish in the flour, shaking off any excess. Add the fish, working in batches, to the hot oil and fry, turning occasionally, until the fish is golden brown and rises to the top of the oil, about 6 minutes. Drain on a paper towel–lined plate.

In a small bowl, whisk together the mayonnaise, relish, and relish juice to make the tartar sauce. Spread it over the bread. Sandwich the fried fish between the bread and serve.

THE GRAVY

Store leftover flour mixture in an airtight container in the refrigerator for future use.

VEGGIES SHOULD BE HEARTY, AND BOLD IN FLAVOR. I LOVE SEASONING VEGGIES JUST AS I WOULD A RACK OF LAMB TO HIGHLIGHT THEIR ALREADY-BRILLIANT AND BOLD TASTE. WHETHER SERVED COOKED OR RAW, VEGGIES ALWAYS SPEAK FOR THEMSELVES . . . JUST LET THEM.

—Lazarus Lynch

TAGGING ALL THE
VEGGIE HATERS
LMAO

VEGGIES AIN'T WHACK

BBQ COLLARD GREEN SALAD WITH CRISPY BACON

SERVES 6 TO 8 **PREP TIME** 5 MINUTES **TOTAL TIME** 20 MINUTES

1 bunch collard greens, stemmed, thick center rib cut out, leaves chopped

Kosher salt

4 slices bacon, diced

½ yellow bell pepper, sliced (about ½ cup)

¼ small red onion, thinly sliced (about ½ cup)

¼ cup your favorite BBQ Sauce (I love something smoky)

¼ cup olive oil

2 tablespoons white vinegar

2 teaspoons Dijon mustard

As a kid, I thought collard greens could only be eaten hot and stewed down with meat, vinegar, and hot sauce. Man, was I missing out on this version. The dressing is killer and, for the most part, store-bought. I served this salad to some friends in Brooklyn with my Sriracha Honey Wings (page 190) and Cornbread That Ain't Sweet (page 178), and not a plate was empty.

Bring a large pot of generously salted water to a boil. Fill a large bowl with ice and water and set it nearby. Add the collard greens to the boiling water and cook until wilted but still bright green, about 2 minutes. Transfer the greens to the ice water. Drain the greens on a paper towel, or spin them in a salad spinner, making sure to squeeze out any excess liquid, and transfer them to a large bowl.

In a large skillet, cook the bacon, stirring occasionally, until crisp, about 10 minutes. Remove with a slotted spoon and transfer to a paper towel–lined plate.

Add the bacon, bell pepper, and onion to the greens.

In a small bowl, whisk together the BBQ sauce, oil, vinegar, and mustard. Pour over the greens, mix, and serve. The longer this sets, the better it gets!

CURRY
CHICKEN PATTIES
(page 63)

BERBERE-SPICED
EGGPLANT
(page 157)

HABANERO BBQ
SHRIMP SKEWERS
(page 224)

GRILLED PEACH, CUCUMBER, <u>AND</u> TOMATO SALAD

SERVES 4 TO 6   **PREP TIME** 5 MINUTES   **TOTAL TIME** 15 MINUTES

2 very ripe peaches, pitted and quartered

1 tablespoon olive oil

½ English cucumber, sliced on an angle (about 1 cup)

8 ounces tricolor cherry tomatoes, halved

¼ cup torn fresh basil or mint leaves, or a mix

Kosher salt and freshly ground black pepper

My family cannot get enough of this salad. What's special about it is the ingredients are ordinary, but when they come together, it's pure magic. It's the simple things that make me happy: a syrupy summer peach, a crisp cucumber, and a juicy, ripe tomato. Can't get enough!

Heat a grill pan over medium-high heat.

Rub the peaches with the oil. Grill the peaches on their two cut sides, turning occasionally, until grill marks appear, 4 to 5 minutes. Transfer the peaches to a large bowl and toss with the cucumber, tomatoes, and basil. Season with salt and pepper to taste. Serve at room temperature.

ASPARAGUS GOT A CRUSH ON POTATO

SERVES 6 **PREP TIME** 10 MINUTES **TOTAL TIME** 30 MINUTES

8 ounces asparagus, trimmed and cut into 2-inch pieces

2 tablespoons plus 2 teaspoons extra-virgin olive oil

Kosher salt and freshly ground black pepper

12 ounces tricolor fingerling potatoes, sliced into ½-inch-thick rounds

1 small shallot, finely chopped

1 tablespoon red wine vinegar

2 teaspoons Dijon mustard

⅓ cup chopped fresh flat-leaf parsley, for serving

Any salad with the word "potato" in it, sign me up! If I were Asparagus, I would have a big crush on Potato. I fell in love with fingerling potatoes in high school. They're naturally buttery, and are great for roasting, grilling, or boiling. This is one of two potato salads in the book. Just an excuse for us all to eat more potatoes.

Preheat the oven to 425°F. Line two baking sheets with parchment paper.

On the first prepared baking sheet, toss the asparagus with 1 teaspoon of the olive oil, ½ teaspoon salt, and ¼ teaspoon pepper and spread the spears out into an even layer. On the second prepared baking sheet, toss potatoes with 1 teaspoon of the olive oil, ½ teaspoon salt, and ¼ teaspoon pepper.

Place both baking sheets in the oven. Roast the asparagus until tender, about 10 minutes, and the potatoes until tender and lightly golden brown, 20 to 25 minutes. Transfer the vegetables to a large bowl.

In a medium bowl, combine the shallot, remaining 2 tablespoons oil, the vinegar, mustard, a pinch each of salt and pepper, and 1 tablespoon water. Whisk until thick and smooth. Pour over the warmed asparagus and potatoes and toss with the parsley. Serve right away.

THE GRAVY

The ends of asparagus are mostly tough and fibrous. To trim, hold the middle and the bottom of the stalk and bend until it snaps. Compost the ends of the asparagus.

CREAMED KALE

SERVES 8 TO 10 **PREP TIME** 10 MINUTES **TOTAL TIME** 45 MINUTES

Kosher salt

2 large bunches kale (about 1½ pounds), ribs and stems removed, leaves chopped into bite-size pieces

1 tablespoon vegetable oil

1 medium yellow onion, chopped

2 garlic cloves, finely chopped

1 tablespoon all-purpose flour

1 quart half-and-half (4 cups)

1 teaspoon sweet paprika

¼ teaspoon cayenne pepper

⅛ teaspoon freshly grated nutmeg

Freshly ground black pepper

I love transforming traditional greens into something more special by smothering them in cream. When I think of creamed greens, I always think of Popeye the Sailor Man—leave it to my childhood. You can taste the love and soul in this recipe. You could substitute kale for any hearty dark green like mustard greens or Swiss chard.

Bring a large pot of salted water to a boil. Fill a large bowl with ice and water and add 1 teaspoon salt; set it nearby. Add the kale to the boiling water and cook until bright green and tender, about 2 minutes. Drain the kale and submerge in the ice water to stop the cooking.

Heat the oil in a large heavy-bottomed pot or Dutch oven over medium-high heat. Add the onion and cook, stirring occasionally, until softened, about 3 minutes. Season lightly with salt. Add the garlic and cook until fragrant, about 1 minute. Stir in the flour and cook for 30 seconds. Stir in half-and-half, breaking up the flour with the back of the spoon, then add the blanched kale, paprika, cayenne, and nutmeg. Reduce the heat to low and bring to a gentle simmer, stirring the greens occasionally. Cook until greens are wilted and tender, 20 to 25 minutes. Season with salt and black pepper to taste. Serve on a fun platter.

CREAMED CORN

3 ears corn, husked

3 tablespoons unsalted butter

1 shallot, finely chopped

2 scallions, finely chopped

2 garlic cloves, finely chopped

Kosher salt

1 cup heavy cream

½ cup freshly grated Parmesan cheese

Freshly ground black pepper

This is such a fun process recipe. Cutting the corn, blending it together, seasoning it . . . so much passion here. Fresh corn must be used to make this recipe for its corn milk. This is a great anytime, any day side dish.

Use a knife to cut the corn kernels away from the cob. Put the kernels in a bowl and set aside. Stand a corn cob in a large dish and use the back of the knife to scrape down cob in an up-and-down motion to release as much corn milk as possible. Repeat with the remaining cobs. Discard the cobs and set the corn with its milk aside.

Melt 2 tablespoons of the butter in a heavy-bottomed pot or Dutch oven over medium heat. Add the shallot, scallions, and garlic and cook stirring occasionally, until softened, about 6 minutes. Season lightly with salt. Add the corn kernels and corn milk and cook, stirring occasionally, for 2 minutes. Add the cream, reduce the heat to medium-low, and bring the mixture to a gentle simmer. Cook until the corn is tender and the cream has thickened, 15 to 20 minutes. Remove from the heat.

Transfer a third of the creamed corn to a blender, add the Parmesan, and puree until smooth. Stir the puree back into the reserved corn mixture along with the remaining 1 tablespoon butter. Season with salt and pepper to taste.

OH-MY-GAH GREEN BEANS WITH CRUSHED PEANUTS

SERVES 6 TO 8   **PREP TIME** 5 MINUTES   **TOTAL TIME** 20 MINUTES

2 tablespoons plus
  2 teaspoons peanut oil

2 tablespoons honey

1 tablespoon rice vinegar

2 teaspoons soy sauce

1 teaspoon toasted
  sesame oil

½ teaspoon crushed red
  pepper flakes

1 large garlic clove,
  finely grated

1 pound Chinese long green
  beans, ends trimmed

½ cup toasted peanuts,
  chopped, for garnish
  (optional)

Kosher salt

¼ cup fresh cilantro, roughly
  chopped, for serving

Hold up! Pull out the wok! I dreamed up this dish in my head, and the first time I made it, I said, "OH-MY-GAH." I don't know about you but the green beans I grew up eating were far from exciting. They either came from a can or were part of a frozen mixed vegetable bag. Can you relate? These beans, however, taste like they were made by your best friend's Chinese grandmother who is gangsta with the Chinese flavors and has been cooking all her life. What I'm saying is, I will never make green beans the same again, ever! These beans will make you say, "OH-MY-GAH!"

In a large bowl, whisk together 2 tablespoons peanut oil, honey, vinegar, soy sauce, sesame oil, red pepper flakes, and garlic. Toss the beans in the sauce and let them marinate, tossing occasionally, for 15 minutes.

If using the peanuts, place them in a dry skillet and toast over medium-high heat, moving them occasionally, until lightly browned and fragrant, 1 to 2 minutes. Transfer the nuts to a nut-safe cutting board or piece of parchment paper and roughly chop.

Heat the remaining 2 teaspoons peanut oil in a large skillet or wok over medium-high heat until smoking, about 3 minutes. Add the green beans with their marinade and cook, tossing often, until hot and bright green, 4 to 5 minutes. Season with salt to taste. Sprinkle the chopped peanuts (if using) and the cilantro on top.

OH-MY-GAH, you can eat it now. ;)

KALE <u>AND</u> BUTTERNUT SQUASH SALAD WITH PAPRIKA BREADCRUMBS <u>AND</u> PARM DRESSING

SERVES 6 **PREP TIME** 10 MINUTES **TOTAL TIME** 40 MINUTES

Two 10-ounce bags frozen diced butternut squash

6 teaspoons plus 1 tablespoon extra-virgin olive oil

½ teaspoon salt, plus more as needed

¼ teaspoon freshly ground black pepper

1 small garlic clove, grated

½ cup panko breadcrumbs

1 teaspoon sweet paprika

¾ cup freshly grated Parmesan cheese

¼ cup sour cream

1 tablespoon fresh lemon juice

2 teaspoons Dijon mustard

1 teaspoon white vinegar

6 cups chopped kale

I grew up thinking salads were iceberg lettuce, tomatoes, and cucumbers with Italian dressing, but they're so much more. Salads should have crunch, acidity, vibrancy, and killer flavor. This salad would be killer with a roasted piece of chicken or duck leg . . . just sayin'. I know duck is being extra, but seriously, this salad might become your go-to lunch on the reg.

Grease a baking sheet with 2 teaspoons olive oil. Place the baking sheet into the oven and preheat the oven to 425°F.

Place the butternut squash into a bowl and toss with 2 teaspoons of the oil, the salt, and pepper. Once the oven is fully preheated, carefully remove the hot baking sheet from the oven and spread the squash evenly on the baking sheet. Roast until the squash is tender and lightly browned, 25 to 30 minutes.

Heat 2 teaspoons of the oil in a medium skillet over medium-high heat. Add the garlic and cook until fragrant, about 1 minute. Add the breadcrumbs and paprika and stir using a wooden spoon, scraping the bottom of the pan. Cook until the breadcrumbs are toasted, about 2 minutes. Transfer to a bowl and add ½ cup of the Parmesan.

In a large bowl, whisk together the sour cream, remaining ¼ cup Parmesan, the lemon juice, remaining 1 tablespoon olive oil, the mustard, and the vinegar. Add the kale and squash and top with the toasted breadcrumbs. Serve right away.

THE GRAVY

You can find frozen chopped butternut squash in your supermarket. I like to heat the baking sheet before roasting to ensure the squash gets beautifully caramelized. If making ahead, prepare all the elements separately in advance, then mix everything together when ready to serve.

JERK-SPICED GRILLED CORN WITH COCONUT CONFETTI

SERVES 8   **PREP TIME** 15 MINUTES   **TOTAL TIME** 25 MINUTES

2 cups unsweetened coconut flakes

Vegetable or canola oil, for grilling

8 ears corn, husked and cut in half

½ cup finely chopped fresh cilantro

½ cup mayonnaise

Juice of 2 limes

2 tablespoons Jerk Dry Rub (recipe follows)

1 lime, cut into wedges

Seriously. Addicted. To. This. Corn. It's next level. There is nothing better than sweet, fresh corn on the cob. Corn is one of my favorite vegetables, up there with potatoes and ketchup! I love smelling the nuttiness of hot corn off the grill on a hot summer day. This corn gets brushed with my jerk-spiced mayo, and then I make it rain toasted coconut! Whoa, I told you, next level!!

Preheat the oven to 400°F and line a baking sheet with parchment paper.

Spread the coconut flakes in an even layer over the prepared baking sheet and bake on the middle rack for 6 to 8 minutes, until lightly golden brown. Set aside.

Heat a grill to medium-high or heat a grill pan over medium-high heat. Brush the grill grates or pan with oil. Brush the corn on all sides with oil and grill, rotating occasionally, until slightly charred on all sides, 10 to 12 minutes total.

Fill a wide, shallow dish with the toasted coconut flakes and cilantro.

In a bowl, mix together the mayonnaise, lime juice, and jerk rub. Brush the cooked corn with the mayonnaise mixture and roll in the coconut mixture to coat all over.

Serve right away with lime wedges.

JERK DRY RUB

MAKES 1 CUP
TOTAL TIME: 5 MINUTES

½ cup allspice

¼ cup kosher salt

1 tablespoon mustard powder

1 tablespoon minced garlic

1 tablespoon granulated sugar

1 tablespoon dark brown sugar

1½ teaspoons cayenne pepper

1 teaspoon chili powder

1 teaspoon crushed red pepper flakes

1 teaspoon dried cilantro

1 teaspoon dried thyme

1 teaspoon freshly ground black pepper

In a small bowl, mix together the allspice, salt, mustard powder, garlic, sugars, cayenne, chili powder, red pepper flakes, cilantro, thyme, and pepper. Store in an airtight container or mason jar in a cool, dry place for up to 1 month.

For best results, marinate your food with the dry rub for at least 2 hours before cooking.

DAD'S OLD-SCHOOL COLLARD GREENS WITH SMOKED MEAT

SERVES 8 TO 10 **PREP TIME** 20 MINUTES **TOTAL TIME** 2 HOURS 15 MINUTES

3 pounds collard greens (about 3 bunches), trimmed and roughly chopped

2 tablespoons olive oil

1 large yellow onion, finely chopped (about 2 cups)

3 garlic cloves, smashed

1 medium red bell pepper, diced (about 1 cup)

1 pound smoked ham hock or (if we must settle) smoked turkey neck bones

2 quarts low-sodium turkey or chicken stock

1 tablespoon white vinegar

1 tablespoon your favorite hot sauce, plus more for serving

Pinch of packed light brown sugar

Kosher salt and freshly ground black pepper

I wrote a song called "Pass Dem Greens and Dat Cornbread." I could hear The Roots and Cory Henry and The Funk Apostles singing/playing it in my head. That's the chant that comes to mind when I think about the goodness of collard greens. A good collard greens recipe will stand the test of time. Everybody has a different way of making "greens," but the Southern way is always slow and low, usually with a piece of smoked or cured meat. Dad made his with either smoked ham hock or turkey necks, bell peppers, and hot sauce. This is how I make it.

To clean the greens, fill the sink or a large bowl with cold water and submerge the greens for about 10 minutes, moving them occasionally. Allow the sand and dirt to fall to the bottom of the sink or bowl completely before removing the greens. Remove the greens and dry them in a salad spinner or on paper towel.

Heat the oil in a large pot over medium heat. Add the onion and garlic and cook, stirring occasionally, until softened, about 2 minutes. Add the bell pepper and cook, stirring occasionally, until softened, about 3 minutes. Add the greens, ham hock, and stock and bring to a boil. Add the vinegar, hot sauce, brown sugar, 1 tablespoon salt, and ½ teaspoon black pepper. Reduce the heat to maintain a simmer, cover, and cook until the greens are tender and dark green, about 1 hour 30 minutes. Season to taste with more salt and black pepper and serve with a dose of hot sauce.

THE GRAVY

You can get ham hock or turkey neck bones at your local grocery store or from a butcher. If you're making your greens ahead, you can store them in the refrigerator for up to 5 days or freeze them for up to 1 month. To thaw, place them in a large pot, add ½ cup water, and cover. Bring to a simmer, stirring occasionally. Adjust seasonings with salt, pepper, and hot sauce.

BEET UP DEM BRUSSELS SPROUTS WITH QUINOA

SERVES 4 **PREP TIME** 15 MINUTES **TOTAL TIME** 1 HOUR 40 MINUTES

2 large beets

4 tablespoons extra-virgin olive oil

Flaky sea salt and freshly ground black pepper

½ pound Brussels sprouts, trimmed and halved

½ cup cooked quinoa, made according to box directions

½ cup pecans, toasted and roughly chopped (optional)

2 scallions, chopped

¼ cup roughly chopped fresh flat-leaf parsley

¼ cup fresh mint leaves

2 tablespoons fresh lemon juice

I decided to add this recipe on the fly with my editor, Lucia Watson. We felt like we wanted a lighter salad to balance out all the other ones. The irony of this salad is that it is the epitome of my two most hated vegetables as a kid: Brussels sprouts and beets. There are two reasons why people hate these veggies: One, you're cooking them wrong, or two, someone is cooking them wrong for you. This salad is up there with my favorite recipes because it truly is light, fresh, and hearty. I could and would eat an entire bowl of this salad with joy. Would I ever serve you something I wouldn't first eat and approve myself? Heck no.

Preheat the oven to 425°F. Line a baking sheet with parchment paper.

Wrap the beets tightly in aluminum foil and place them on an unlined rimmed baking sheet. Roast until the beets are tender and easily pierced with a knife, about 1 hour 10 minutes.

On the parchment-lined baking sheet, toss the Brussels sprouts, 1 tablespoon of the oil, ½ teaspoon salt, and ¼ teaspoon pepper. Roast until golden brown and tender, about 25 minutes. Transfer to a large bowl and let cool.

Place the Brussels sprouts and quinoa in a large bowl.

Put on gloves (so your hands don't look like a crime scene) and remove the beets from the aluminum foil. Run them under cold water to cool, then peel the skins off using a paper towel. Cover cutting board with parchment paper and slice the beets into wedges, then add them to the bowl with the sprouts and quinoa. Stir in the pecans (if using), scallions, parsley, mint, lemon juice, and remaining 3 tablespoons olive oil. Toss and season to taste with salt and pepper. Serve at room temperature.

DAD'S CREAMY COLESLAW

SERVES 6 TO 8 **PREP TIME** 10 MINUTES **TOTAL TIME** 2 HOURS 10 MINUTES

1 small head green cabbage, shredded (about 1 cup)

2 large carrots, shredded (about 1 cup)

½ red bell pepper, finely diced

½ green bell pepper, finely diced

1 cup mayonnaise

2 tablespoons Dijon mustard

2 tablespoons pickle juice (from a jar of pickles)

2 teaspoons pickle relish

2 teaspoons sugar

½ teaspoon kosher salt

½ teaspoon freshly ground black pepper

This is my favorite! Dad used to make huge pans of coleslaw at the restaurant. It was one of his most popular sides. He didn't have a food processor, so he shredded all the cabbage and carrots by hand. That was the way his mother showed him how to make it. I'm so glad he passed this one down to me. It's everything coleslaw should be: creamy but not runny, a little crunchy, and perfectly sweet and tangy. The flavors meld as they sit, and taste better and better. I top my Shorty's Short Rib Sliders (page 119) with this coleslaw for reasons only tasting it could explain. You're gonna want to pass this one down to your folks, too.

In a large bowl, mix together all the ingredients before the mayo.

In a medium bowl, whisk together the mayo, mustard, pickle juice, relish, sugar, salt, and black pepper. Pour the mayo mixture over the cabbage mixture and toss.

Cover and refrigerate for at least 2 hours before serving. This will keep for up to 1 week.

THE GRAVY

Recipes like this one make me very grateful to have a food processor with a shredder attachment. If you don't have one, shredding by hand works, too (like Dad did). You could even cheat this recipe, save time, and buy a 16-ounce packaged, ready-to-eat coleslaw mix. I won't judge you.

CREAMY POTATO SALAD WITH JALAPEÑO AND BACON

SERVES 8 TO 10 **PREP TIME** 15 MINUTES **TOTAL TIME** 50 MINUTES

2 pounds Yukon gold potatoes, peeled and cut into 1-inch cubes (about 8 cups)

Kosher salt

4 thick-cut slices bacon, diced

¾ cup mayonnaise

1 tablespoon Dijon mustard

Juice of 1 lemon

1 jalapeño, seeded and finely diced

2 tablespoons chopped fresh dill

2 tablespoons chopped fresh flat-leaf parsley

½ teaspoon freshly ground black pepper

This is Potato Salad No. 2. It's a new and fresh take on the potato salad of my childhood. I first made this recipe for a YouTube video right before the Fourth of July and was surprised to see how well it was received. It's creamy, spicy, and wonderfully salty (thank you, bacon). I'm glad this one made the book!

Put the potatoes in a large pot and cover with cold water. Season potatoes with 1 tablespoon salt and bring the water to a boil. Cook the potatoes until just under fork-tender (they should still have a little firmness), about 25 minutes. Drain the potatoes in a colander in the sink. Cover the colander with a clean kitchen towel for about 15 minutes, until cooled.

In a medium skillet, cook the bacon over medium heat, stirring occasionally, until crisp, about 8 minutes. Drain the bacon onto a paper towel–lined plate.

In a medium bowl, stir together the mayonnaise, mustard, lemon juice, jalapeño, dill, parsley, and pepper. Add the potatoes and bacon and toss until fully coated. Season with salt and pepper to taste.

Serve at room temperature or store in an airtight container in the refrigerator for up to 5 days.

THE GRAVY

Whenever working with hot peppers, use gloves, and wash hands with dish soap right after to prevent skin irritation or burning (I've got some horror stories, LOL.) Use as little or as much jalapeño as you want in this recipe. Some jalapeños are spicier than others. You could substitute Yukon gold potatoes for yellow or red-skinned potatoes.

ROASTED CAULIFLOWER WITH HAPPY SALSA

SERVES 6 **PREP TIME** 10 MINUTES **TOTAL TIME** 30 MINUTES

CAULIFLOWER

1 small head cauliflower,
cut into florets

2 tablespoons extra-virgin
olive oil

1 teaspoon fresh thyme
leaves

½ teaspoon dried oregano

1 lemon

Kosher salt and freshly
ground black pepper

HAPPY SALSA

1 large heirloom tomato,
roughly chopped,
about 1 cup

½ cup shelled pistachios,
toasted

½ cup roughly chopped fresh
flat-leaf parsley

½ cup fresh basil leaves

¼ cup extra-virgin olive oil

1 small garlic clove,
finely grated

¼ teaspoon salt

Roasted cauliflower is a beautiful thing for so many reasons. Roasting brings out the natural sugars in foods and makes them tastier. Cauliflower ain't no punk, and it can stand up to high-heat cooking. I call this my happy salsa, because it's vibrant and full of life, which makes me happy. I promise, you will love.

Make the cauliflower: Preheat the oven to 475°F.

On a baking sheet, toss together the cauliflower, oil, thyme, oregano, ½ teaspoon lemon zest, ½ teaspoon salt, and ½ teaspoon pepper. Roast until the florets are tender and their tops are golden, about 15 minutes. Let cool, then transfer to a platter.

Make the happy salsa: In the bowl of a food processor, combine the tomato, pistachios, parsley, basil, oil, 1 teaspoon lemon zest, 1 teaspoon lemon juice, garlic, and salt. Pulse a few times, keeping the texture.

Serve the happy salsa over the cauliflower!

BERBERE-SPICED EGGPLANT

SERVES 6 TO 8 **PREP TIME** 15 MINUTES **TOTAL TIME** 40 MINUTES

½ cup extra-virgin olive oil, plus more for the grill

¾ cup nonfat Greek yogurt

4 tablespoons chopped fresh cilantro, divided

3 tablespoons berbere seasoning

2 garlic cloves, minced

Kosher salt and freshly ground black pepper

1 large eggplant, sliced lengthwise into ½-inch-thick pieces

1 tablespoon fresh lemon juice

I studied abroad in Kigali, Rwanda, my freshman year of college. On the way there, we had a layover in Ethiopia, where I was properly introduced to berbere. Berbere (pronounced BUR-BERRY, like the fashion brand) is a wild Ethiopian spice mixture of chile peppers, garlic, fenugreek, and other spices. I had never heard of it before. It was on my chicken and yogurt sauce, on my vegetables and rice—it was in the air. I fell in love with berbere, and now it's part of my family. I love it on anything, especially grilled fish or fire-roasted eggplant!

Heat the grill to medium-high heat and rub the grates with oil.

In a wide, shallow dish, whisk together the oil, ½ cup of the yogurt, 2 tablespoons of the cilantro, 2 tablespoons of the berbere seasoning, the garlic, ½ teaspoon salt, and ½ teaspoon pepper.

Massage the eggplant pieces with the yogurt mixture on all sides and let stand for 5 minutes. Grill the eggplant, turning occasionally, until tender and golden brown on both sides, 8 to 10 minutes total.

In a small bowl, mix together the remaining ¼ cup yogurt, remaining 1 tablespoon Berbere seasoning, ¼ teaspoon salt, and the lemon juice.

Serve the eggplant on a platter and drizzle with the yogurt sauce. Garnish with the remaining cilantro.

THE GRAVY

If you can't find berbere at your supermarket (which is likely), you can shop for it online at penzeys.com and amazon.com. And if you're thinking, "What else could I make with berbere?" you can add it to your taco meat, barbecued ribs and sauces, roasted veggies, and meatballs. Once you taste it, you'll be using it on everything!

FUN ROASTED VEGGIES

Roasting veggies is the easiest way to cook them. You just oil them up, season, roast, and they're done. Here are a bunch of easy-peasy (no pun intended) roasted veggies.

BRUSSELS SPROUTS

1½ pounds Brussels sprouts, trimmed and halved

2 tablespoons extra-virgin olive oil

Kosher salt and freshly ground black pepper

Preheat the oven to 400°F. Line a baking sheet with parchment paper.

Toss the Brussels sprouts on the prepared baking sheet with the olive oil and ¼ teaspoon each of salt and pepper. Roast until very golden brown, 25 to 30 minutes. Season with additional salt and pepper to taste.

JAZZ IT UP *Fried garlic, chopped bacon pieces*

CARROTS

2 pounds carrots, quartered lengthwise

2 tablespoons extra-virgin olive oil

Kosher salt and freshly ground black pepper

Preheat the oven to 400°F. Line a baking sheet with parchment paper.

Toss the carrots on the prepared baking sheet with the olive oil and ½ teaspoon each of salt and pepper. Roast until tender and golden brown, 25 to 30 minutes. Season with additional salt and pepper to taste.

JAZZ IT UP *Berbere spice, ground cinnamon, ground cumin, ground coriander, ground allspice, parsley*

ASPARAGUS

1 pound asparagus, tough ends snapped off

1 tablespoon extra-virgin olive oil

Kosher salt and freshly ground black pepper

Preheat the oven to 400°F. Line a baking sheet with parchment paper.

Toss the asparagus on the prepared baking sheet with the olive oil and ¼ teaspoon each of salt and pepper. Roast until tender, 15 to 20 minutes. Season with additional salt and pepper to taste.

JAZZ IT UP *Grated Parmesan cheese, toasted panko breadcrumbs, fresh basil*

PARSNIPS

1 pound parsnips

2 tablespoons extra-virgin olive oil

Kosher salt and freshly ground black pepper

Preheat the oven to 450°F. Line a baking sheet with parchment paper.

Toss the parsnips on the prepared baking sheet with the olive oil and ¼ teaspoon each of salt and pepper. Roast until very golden brown, 20 to 25 minutes. Season with additional salt and pepper to taste.

JAZZ IT UP *Ground coriander, ground cumin, sumac, chopped parsley, ground fennel*

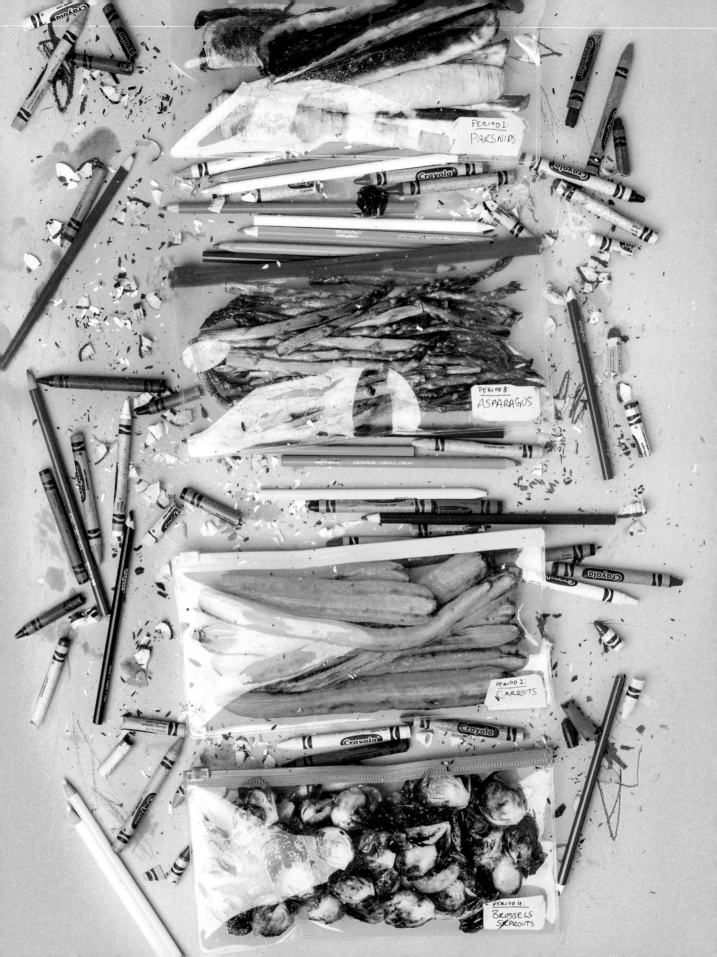

WORTHINESS IS AT THE CORE
OF LIVING A LIFE
OF PURPOSE AND FULFILLMENT.
YOU ARE WORTHY OF
RESPECT, COMPASSION, AND
KINDNESS. YOU ARE WORTHY
OF SELF-APPRECIATION, JOY,
AND SELF-LOVE.

YOU ARE WORTHY OF BEING TREATED

WITH DIGNITY AND HUMANITY.
MAKE NO APOLOGIES AND
WALK IN YOUR WORTHINESS.

—*Lazarus Lynch*

FLAWLESS CARBS

DAD'S MAC AND CHEESE

SERVES 10 TO 12   **PREP TIME** 20 MINUTES   **TOTAL TIME** 1 HOUR

4 tablespoons (½ stick) unsalted butter, melted and cooled, plus more for greasing

Kosher salt

1 pound elbow macaroni

2 large eggs

One (12-ounce) can Carnation evaporated milk

2 teaspoons adobo with garlic seasoning

1 teaspoon freshly ground black pepper

8 ounces sharp cheddar cheese, shredded

8 ounces pepper Jack cheese, shredded

8 ounces whole-milk mozzarella cheese, shredded

Here's THE ultimate mac and cheese recipe. If you've ever tasted my dad's mac and cheese, you've died and come back.

Dad made pans of mac and cheese at the restaurant, and even more pans at home during the holidays. His was like the brick version of mac and cheese that stands up, like the Great Wall of China. I once heard that you can tell a good soul food joint from a not-so-good soul food joint if they run out of mac n cheese. Say what you want, Pops would always run out of mac and cheese. This book would not be Son of a Southern Chef without this recipe. It's a must try. It doesn't get any more real than this.

Preheat the oven to 375°F. Grease a 9 x 13-inch baking dish with butter.

Bring a pot of salted water to a boil and add the pasta. Cook for 3 minutes less than what the box suggests. Drain and rinse the pasta under cold water to stop the cooking. Drain again, then set aside.

In a large bowl, whisk together the eggs, evaporated milk, adobo, pepper, and 4 tablespoons butter. Pour in the noodles and coat evenly with the egg mixture.

Mix the cheddar, pepper Jack, and mozzarella together in a bowl.

Pour one-third of the pasta over the bottom of the prepared dish. Sprinkle with one-third of the cheese mixture. Repeat to make two more layers, ending with the cheese on top. Bake until the top is golden brown, about 20 minutes. Let cool for 5 minutes before serving (if you can stand it)!

NO-BOIL MAC AND CHEESE WITH HAM **AND** GREENS

SERVES 12 **PREP TIME** 10 MINUTES **TOTAL TIME** 45 MINUTES

3 tablespoons unsalted butter, at room temperature

Kosher salt

1 cup collard greens, cooked or raw

1 pound elbow macaroni

1 cup chopped cooked ham

1 cup shredded sharp cheddar cheese

1 cup freshly grated Parmesan cheese

½ cup shredded Swiss cheese

½ cup shredded Gruyère cheese

Freshly ground black pepper

4 cups heavy cream

½ cup crushed Ritz Garlic Butter crackers (½ sleeve)

2 tablespoons chopped fresh flat-leaf parsley

2 garlic cloves, chopped

THE GRAVY

You could substitute the collards for any other green and mushrooms or roasted chicken for ham.

No-boil? Crazy, right? I shared this recipe for a Thanksgiving segment on the *Today* show! The next day, people were making this recipe all over the country, and even in Germany (no lie). The beauty of this recipe is that it's designed for the lazy and the busy. You don't even have to boil the noodles, and you can add leftovers to make the old feel new. Grandma and dem would be shook!

Preheat the oven to 400°F. Grease a 9 x 13-inch baking dish with 1 tablespoon of the butter.

Bring a large pot of salted water to a boil. Add the collard greens and cook until tender and bright green, about 3 minutes. Drain and rinse the greens under cold water to stop the cooking. Drain again, then set aside.

In the prepared baking dish, toss the pasta with the collard greens, ham, ½ cup of the cheddar, ½ cup of the Parmesan, ¼ cup of the Swiss, and ¼ cup of the Gruyère, 2 teaspoons salt, and 1 teaspoon pepper.

In a large pot, bring the heavy cream to a rolling boil over medium-high heat. When cream begins to bubble up, shut off heat. Pour the hot cream over the mixture to completely submerge the pasta. Cover with aluminum foil and bake until the pasta is almost tender, about 25 minutes.

Melt the remaining 2 tablespoons butter in the microwave.

In a large bowl, combine the melted butter with the Ritz crackers, remaining ½ cup cheddar, ½ cup Parmesan, ¼ cup Swiss, ¼ cup Gruyère, the parsley, and the garlic. Season lightly with salt and pepper. Remove the foil and sprinkle the crumbs evenly over the top. Bake until the pasta is completely tender, the cheese is bubbling, and the top is golden brown, about 10 minutes more. Remove the dish from the oven and let stand for 10 minutes before serving. Serve right away.

RICE AND PEAS

SERVES 6 TO 8   **PREP TIME** 1 HOUR 20 MINUTES   **TOTAL TIME** 1 HOUR 45 MINUTES

1 cup dried red kidney beans, rinsed and drained

6½ cups low-sodium chicken stock

2 cups uncooked parboiled rice, rinsed and drained

¼ cup grated Grace Pure Creamed Coconut or other unsweetened coconut block

3 fresh thyme sprigs

1 habanero pepper

½ teaspoon kosher salt

¼ teaspoon ground allspice

You cannot eat jerk chicken or oxtails without rice and peas; it's a law. Rice and peas sound like two different dishes, but it's actually just one dish. We are big rice eaters in my home and have a running joke: *"What is dinner without rice?"* The Caribbean cooks I know can make rice and peas in their sleep because they've been making it for so long. It's taken me a while to master this recipe; however, the general rule of thumb for cooking rice is NO peeking into the pot, or else steam will escape and the rice won't cook perfectly.

Put the beans and 4 cups of the stock in a medium Dutch oven or saucepot and soak, covered, overnight.

Bring the beans and stock to a full boil and boil for 15 minutes. Reduce the heat to medium-low and simmer the beans until tender, about 1 hour.

Add the remaining 2½ cups stock and bring to a boil. Using a fork, stir in the rice, grated creamed coconut, thyme, habanero, salt, and allspice and cover the pot with a tight-fitting lid. Reduce the heat to low and cook until the rice is tender, about 20 minutes. Turn off the heat and let stand, covered, for 5 minutes. Remove the thyme and habanero. Fluff the rice, separating the grains with a fork, and serve.

THE GRAVY

You must use parboiled rice for this recipe. Other rice grains just won't work. If you've ever made a mushy pot of rice, there is hope for recovery. Spread the rice rice on a baking sheet and place it in a preheated 200°F oven until it dries out. This has saved me and many hungry bellies many times!

Quick-soak dried beans method: Bring the water and beans to a full boil for 2 minutes. Remove from the heat, cover with a lid, and let the beans stand for 1 hour. Ready to use.

BROWN BUTTER CANDIED YAM MASH WITH GOAT CHEESE BRÛLÉE

SERVES 6 TO 8 **PREP TIME** 1 HOUR 10 MINUTES **TOTAL TIME** 1 HOUR 5 MINUTES

5 large orange sweet potatoes, peeled and cut into 1-inch cubes

Kosher salt and freshly ground black pepper

½ cup (1 stick) unsalted butter

⅔ cup packed light brown sugar

¼ cup granulated sugar

½ teaspoon grated orange zest

Juice of 1 orange, strained (about ½ cup)

Couple splashes of hot sauce

1 teaspoon ground cinnamon

⅛ teaspoon ground allspice

Pinch freshly grated nutmeg

1 cup marshmallows

⅔ cup creamy fresh goat cheese, at room temperature

I love me some candied yams. For those who are unfamiliar, candied yams are not actually yams. They're sweet potatoes that have been glazed in a sugary syrup, often with butter, sugar, and spices like cinnamon and nutmeg. I go chefy here with the brown butter and goat cheese, but trust me, they are as good as the traditional. You may even like them more.

Bring a large pot of water to a boil. Add the potatoes and a little salt to the water. Cook until the potatoes are fork-tender, about 25 minutes. Drain the potatoes.

Preheat oven to 375°F. Place oven rack in the middle of the oven.

Make the brown butter: Melt the butter in a medium saucepan over medium-high heat until butter turns brown in color and smells nutty, 6 to 8 minutes. Transfer to a heatproof bowl and set aside.

Transfer the potatoes to an ovenproof casserole dish. Pour the melted butter on top, the sugars, orange zest, orange juice, hot sauce, cinnamon, allspice, and nutmeg, and toss together. Roast in the oven until the potatoes become candied and the glaze thickens and potatoes slightly brown, about 20 minutes.

Remove dish from the oven and mash the candied yams with a potato masher or the back of a fork. Set oven to broil.

Put the marshmallows in a microwave-safe bowl and microwave on high in 20-second intervals, stirring between each interval, until the marshmallows are fully melted, 1 minute or less total. Stir in the goat cheese until the mixture is smooth, then spread the mixture over the candied yams. Broil until the cheese is lightly browned, about 2 minutes. Keep your eyes and nose open in case this happens faster. Remove yams from the oven and stir the goat cheese mixture into the sweet potatoes in a swirl pattern using a knife or chopstick. Serve warm.

THANKSGIVING STUFFING WITH APPLES AND CHORIZO

SERVES 10 TO 12 PREP TIME 15 MINUTES TOTAL TIME 1 HOUR 15 MINUTES

4 tablespoons unsalted butter, at room temperature

6 cups cubed day-old cornbread

1 medium yellow onion, diced (about 1 cup)

1 Golden Delicious apple, peeled, cored, and diced (about 1 cup)

3 celery stalks, small diced (about 1 cup)

1 red bell pepper, diced (about 1 cup)

1 green bell pepper, diced (about 1 cup)

2 tablespoons chopped fresh flat-leaf parsley

1 tablespoon fresh thyme leaves

1 teaspoon poultry seasoning

10 ounces Spanish chorizo sausage, diced

½ cup dry white wine

1 cup low-sodium chicken stock

½ cup golden raisins

½ cup chopped toasted walnuts (optional)

½ teaspoon kosher salt

¼ teaspoon freshly ground black pepper

Even though this recipe is called "Thanksgiving Stuffing," you can eat it in the middle of March if you really want to. No shade to the box stuffing, but there's nothing like a stuffing made from scratch. My dad used to make his stuffing with Jiffy, chicken gizzards, sausage, and a pinch of sugar. I start mine using day-old Cornbread That Ain't Sweet (page 178), usually with chopped herbs tossed inside. Then, I assemble the stuffing the next day. Feel free to change this recipe up and make this the stuffing of your dreams. Just don't call it my recipe, LOL.

Preheat the oven to 375°F. Grease a deep 9 x 13-inch casserole dish with 1 tablespoon of the butter.

Put the cornbread in a large bowl.

Melt 3 tablespoons of the butter in a large pot over medium heat. Add the onion and apple and cook, stirring occasionally, until tender, about 5 minutes. Add the celery and bell peppers and cook, stirring occasionally, until tender, 5 to 7 minutes. Shut off the heat and stir in the parsley, thyme, and poultry seasoning. Transfer the mixture to the bowl with the cornbread.

In the same pan, cook the chorizo over medium-high heat until browned on all sides. Add the wine and cook until evaporated, about 5 minutes. Transfer the sausage to the bowl with cornbread mixture. Add the stock, raisins, walnuts (if using), salt, and black pepper and gently toss everything together. Transfer to the prepared baking dish and bake the stuffing until browned on top and hot in the middle, 30 to 40 minutes. Let rest for about 10 minutes before serving.

THE GRAVY

If you need to make a quick, same-day stuffing, make the cornbread on a rimmed baking sheet and let cool. Slice the cornbread into cubes, then toast the cubes in a preheated 400°F oven until crunchy, about 10 minutes. Cool the cubes and it's ret-to-go.

MY MESSY BBQ BAKED BEANS

SERVES 4   **PREP TIME** 5 MINUTES   **TOTAL TIME** 40 MINUTES

5 slices smoked bacon, chopped

1 yellow onion, finely chopped (about 1 cup)

4 garlic cloves, chopped

Four (15-ounce) cans great northern beans, drained and rinsed

1½ cups low-sodium chicken stock, plus more as desired

¼ cup lightly packed dark brown sugar

3 tablespoons apple cider vinegar

2 tablespoons ketchup

2 tablespoons yellow mustard

1 tablespoon dark molasses

2 teaspoons chili powder

¼ teaspoon kosher salt

Me and baked beans go way back to the days when I ate them out of a can. Okay, I'm still obsessed with baked beans (even from the can) and these are so easy to throw together. Mom used to make us an English breakfast with fried sunnyside up eggs, sausage, and, you guessed it, baked beans. I want them on top of my burgers (because I'm not a hot dog fan), next to my cole slaw, and near to my Dr Pepper Up My Sesame Ribs (page 215).

Preheat the oven to 400°F.

In a Dutch oven, cook the bacon over medium-high heat until the fat has rendered and the bacon is crisp, 6 to 8 minutes. Add the onion and garlic and cook, stirring occasionally, until softened, about 5 minutes. Stir in the beans, stock, brown sugar, vinegar, ketchup, mustard, molasses, chili powder, and salt. Transfer the pot to the oven and bake, uncovered, until the beans are saucy and thick, about 30 minutes.

Carefully remove from the oven and stir. For a looser consistency, add more stock, ¼ cup at a time. Serve.

AIN'T THAT EASY . . . ROTI

SERVES 6 **PREP TIME** 10 MINUTES **TOTAL TIME** 1 HOUR 30 MINUTES

- 5 cups all-purpose flour, plus more as needed
- 1 teaspoon garlic powder (optional)
- 1 teaspoon kosher salt
- ½ teaspoon baking powder
- 1 cup canola oil, plus more for brushing

Every culture has its own claim-to-fame bread. The French have baguette. The Greeks have pita. The Italians have focaccia. And the Guyanese have roti. My mother used to buy roti from the bakery (she still does), but nowadays we make them ourselves. The best way to eat roti is with your hands. Tear up the roti, mop up the curry, and devour. Making fresh roti from scratch might seem intimidating, but it's a lot of fun. The best part of making this recipe is "clapping" the roti—more on this later. See pages 176–177 for steps.

In a large bowl or the bowl of a stand mixer fitted with the dough hook, mix together 4 cups of the flour, the garlic powder (if using), salt, and baking powder. Pour in 1½ cups room-temperature water and mix to form a dough. Knead the dough 6 to 8 times to form a smooth, soft, and elastic ball. Sprinkle in up to 1 tablespoon more flour if needed to reach the desired consistency.

On a floured surface, roll the dough into a 12-inch-long log, then divide it into 8 even pieces. Roll each piece into a 6-inch round, brush with oil, and sprinkle with flour. Cut the dough from the center to the edge, and roll up one end to the next in a cone-like shape. Tuck the flaps of dough into the center and turn the dough upside down. Push down the center of the opposite side of the dough and flatten it into a round disc. Cover the dough with plastic wrap and shape the remaining pieces of dough. Allow the dough to rest for 30 minutes.

Fill a bowl with the oil. Put the remaining 1 cup flour in a shallow bowl.

Heat a 10-inch skillet over medium-high heat.

Roll each dough piece in the flour. Roll out the dough into an 8-inch round, ⅛ inch thick. Cook the roti on one side for 30 seconds. Using your hand or tongs, flip the roti. Dip a paper towel into the bowl of oil and brush the top of the roti with oil-coated paper towel. Cook for 15 seconds more, then flip again and brush with more oil. The roti will begin to puff up. Cook for

THE GRAVY

Clapping the roti between your hands about ten times releases the air pockets and makes the roti flaky. For-real roti makers never use a towel, just their hands, even though it burns like hell. But you can use a towel.

15 seconds, flip one more time (the roti should have brown spots on it), and cook for a final 15 seconds. Remove the roti from the pan, fold it in half, and set aside on a plate. Repeat to cook all the rotis, one at a time, stacking the finished ones on top of the others.

Place one roti at a time in a clean kitchen towel and clap the roti between your hands until it begins to flake. Do this in an open area, as it can get messy. Repeat with the remaining rotis and keep covered with a kitchen towel until ready to serve.

Serve the rotis same day or wrap tightly in plastic wrap and store for up to 1 day.

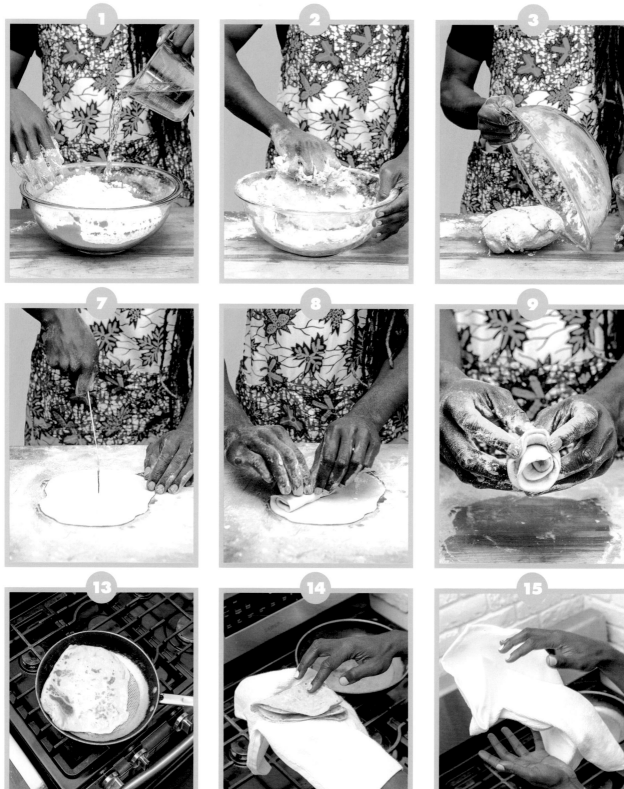

CORNBREAD THAT AIN'T SWEET

vs.

CORNBREAD THAT TASTES LIKE CAKE

I am a cornbread FANATIC. I could eat an entire pan by myself (and I have) . . . Because of the overwhelming opinions for or against sweet cornbread vs. savory, I decided to give you both. I'll let y'all fight it out. I use 1 tablespoon leftover bacon fat to grease my skillet, okurrr!!

CORNBREAD THAT AIN'T SWEET

SERVES 10 TO 12
PREP TIME: 15 MINUTES
TOTAL TIME: 45 MINUTES

This cornbread is dope with Dad's Old-School Collard Greens (page 00) or by itself. Do as you wish!

½ cup (1 stick) unsalted butter

1 cup stone-ground yellow cornmeal

⅔ cup all-purpose flour

2 teaspoons sugar

¼ teaspoon baking powder

½ teaspoon baking soda

½ teaspoon kosher salt

¾ cup buttermilk

2 large eggs, lightly beaten

Kernels from 2 ears corn (about 1½ cups)

1 jalapeño, seeded and chopped

1 cup shredded pepper Jack cheese (about 4 ounces)

2 tablespoons honey

1 tablespoon canned chipotle peppers in adobo sauce

Preheat the oven to 425°F.

Melt 6 tablespoons of the butter in a 10-inch cast-iron skillet over medium heat, swirling the pan occasionally to grease the sides of the skillet. Transfer the melted butter to a heatproof bowl and place the skillet in the oven.

In a large bowl, whisk together the cornmeal, flour, sugar, baking powder, baking soda, and salt. Whisk in the buttermilk, eggs, and melted butter and stir to thoroughly combine. Fold in the corn kernels, jalapeño, and cheese.

Carefully remove the hot skillet from the oven and pour the batter into the skillet. Return the skillet to the oven and bake the cornbread until the top is golden brown and a toothpick comes out clean, about 25 minutes.

Melt the remaining 2 tablespoons of butter. Stir in the honey and chipotle. Pour the honey butter onto the hot cornbread and spread over the top before slicing. Serve warm.

CORNBREAD THAT TASTES LIKE CAKE

SERVES 10 TO 12
PREP TIME: 10 MINUTE
TOTAL TIME: 35 MINUTES

For all who want sweet cornbread . . . your prayers have been answered. You're welcome.

6 tablespoons (¾ stick) unsalted butter, plus more for serving

⅔ cup sugar

1 cup stone-ground yellow cornmeal

¾ cup all-purpose flour

1¼ teaspoons baking powder

½ teaspoon baking soda

¾ teaspoon kosher salt

¾ cup buttermilk

2 large eggs, lightly beaten

Preheat the oven to 425°F.

Melt the butter in a 10-inch cast-iron skillet over medium heat, swirling the pan occasionally to grease the sides of the skillet. Transfer to a heatproof bowl. Set the skillet in the oven.

In a large bowl, whisk together the sugar, cornmeal, flour, baking powder, baking soda, and salt. Whisk in the buttermilk and eggs. Add the butter and stir to combine.

Pour the batter into the hot skillet and bake the cornbread until the top is golden brown and a toothpick inserted into the center comes out clean, about 20 minutes.

Serve warm with butter.

COOKING, FOR ME, WAS ALWAYS COMMUNAL—DONE BY THE MASSES AND SHARED WITH PEOPLE YOU LOVE.

WHETHER IT WAS BIG SUNDAY FEASTS, OR SHARING A TWENTY-PIECE BUCKET OF NEW YORK FRIED CHICKEN WITH MY SIBLINGS, GOOD FOOD AND GOOD COOKING WERE ALWAYS A PART OF MY LIFE, AND I WAS TAUGHT TO APPRECIATE IT. I RELIVE THESE INCREDIBLE MEMORIES EVERY TIME I PULL OUT AN OLD FAMILY RECIPE.

—Lazarus Lynch

BIRDS ON FLEEK

BROWN STEW CHICKEN

SERVES 5 OR 6 **PREP TIME** 1 HOUR **TOTAL TIME** 4 HOURS

1 cup diced yellow onion

1 bunch scallions, chopped

4 garlic cloves, minced

2 teaspoons packed dark brown sugar

1 teaspoon browning sauce (see page 18)

2 or 3 sprigs fresh thyme, chopped

½ teaspoon sweet paprika

¼ teaspoon ground ginger

¼ teaspoon chili powder

Kosher salt and freshly ground black pepper

8 boneless, skinless chicken pieces

3 tablespoons canola or vegetable oil

4 cups low-sodium chicken stock

2 carrots, sliced

1 ripe tomato, chopped (about ½ cup)

½ cup ketchup

½ teaspoon ground allspice

3 dried bay leaves

Rice and Peas (page 167), for serving

I grew up around a lot of Jamaicans and a lot of brown stew chicken. I live for the brown stew gravy soaking into my rice and peas. Everyone makes their brown stew a little differently, but this is the way I learned from watching my Jamaican relatives. It is spot on!

In a gallon-size plastic storage bag, combine the onion, scallions, garlic, brown sugar, browning sauce, thyme, paprika, ginger, chili powder, 1 teaspoon salt, and ½ teaspoon pepper. Add the chicken and massage the marinade into the chicken, tossing well to evenly coat. Seal the bag and refrigerate for 2 hours or up to overnight.

Line a baking sheet with parchment paper. Remove the chicken pieces from the marinade and lay them on the baking sheet. Pat off excess marinade with paper towels. Set aside for about 10 minutes. Reserve marinade.

Heat the oil in a large heavy-bottomed pot or Dutch oven over medium-high heat until hot, about 5 minutes. Working in batches if needed, add the chicken to the hot oil and fry, turning it occasionally, until deep golden brown on all sides, about 10 minutes total.

Once all chicken pieces are bolden brown, stir in the stock, reserved marinade, the carrots, tomato, ketchup, allspice, and bay leaves.

Cover the pot and bring the mixture to a boil, about 10 minutes. Remove the lid and reduce the heat to low. Cover and cook until the chicken is very tender and the sauce has reduced by half, about 45 minutes. Season with salt and pepper to taste. Remove the bay leaves.

Serve the chicken with rice and peas.

RICE AND PEAS
(page 167)

YOU IS A BIRD, FRIED CHICKEN WITH GRAVY

SERVES 4 OR 5 **PREP TIME** 15 MINUTES **TOTAL TIME** 3 HOURS 30 MINUTES

FRIED CHICKEN

1 cup buttermilk

2 large eggs

2 tablespoons your favorite hot sauce

Kosher salt and freshly ground black pepper

8 to 10 skin-on chicken pieces

2 cups plus 2 tablespoons all-purpose flour

2 tablespoons hot smoked paprika

2 tablespoons onion powder

2 tablespoons garlic powder

1 tablespoon packed dark brown sugar

1 tablespoon dried oregano

2 teaspoons cayenne pepper

Canola or peanut oil, for frying

Wait . . . do y'all remember the fried chicken scene from *Precious*? If you don't know what I'm referring to, put this book down right now and YouTube "Precious Fried Chicken Scene." When I tell you #ImWith Precious this scene could not be more real to express my love for the fried bird. Fried chicken is one of those foods that defines the African American experience. My ancestors used to pan-fry chicken in a combination of lard and butter, with a slice of smoked pork for extra flavor. We ain't doing all that. The point is, fried chicken, for generations, has been at the pinnacle of soul food tradition and the black experience. To be fair, fried chicken is universal. Koreans have a wavy fried chicken, and so do the Indian, and the Japanese. No matter where you come from, fried chicken is for us all!

Make the fried chicken: In a large bowl, whisk together the buttermilk, eggs, hot sauce, 2 teaspoons salt, and 2 teaspoons black pepper. Submerge the chicken pieces in the mixture, turning the pieces to coat them evenly. Cover the bowl with plastic wrap and refrigerate for at least 2 hours and up to 24 hours. Remove from the refrigerator at least 30 minutes before cooking.

Preheat the oven to 375°F. Line a baking sheet with aluminum foil and set a wire rack on top.

In a large bowl or resealable bag, combine the flour, paprika, onion powder, garlic powder, brown sugar, oregano, cayenne, and 2 teaspoons salt. Add ¼ cup of the buttermilk brine to the flour mixture and mix with a fork to make clumps. Remove the chicken from the brine, allowing the excess to drip off, and add to the bowl or bag. Toss to coat completely in the flour mixture.

RECIPE AND INGREDIENTS CONTINUE ⟫⟫

GRAVY

3 tablespoons canola oil or unsalted butter

1 shallot, finely chopped

3 tablespoons all-purpose flour

2 cups low-sodium chicken stock

3 sprigs fresh thyme

1 teaspoon chicken bouillon or 1 chicken bouillon cube

A few dashes your favorite hot sauce

Kosher salt and freshly ground black pepper

Fill a 12-inch cast-iron skillet or Dutch oven with oil to a depth of 2 inches and heat over medium-high heat to 360°F. Working in three or four batches, fry the chicken until golden on one side, then flip and fry until golden brown on the second side, about 10 minutes total. Transfer the chicken to the prepared baking sheet and repeat to fry the rest of the chicken pieces. Continue cooking the chicken pieces in the oven until the internal temperature reaches 165°F on a digital thermometer inserted at the thickest part of the chicken, 15 to 20 minutes.

Meanwhile, make the gravy: Heat the 3 tablespoons oil in a medium skillet over medium-high heat. Add the shallot to the pan and cook, stirring, until softened, about 2 minutes. Add the flour and stir to combine. Reduce heat to medium and cook, stirring occasionally, until the flour turns very brown in color, 10 to 12 minutes. (This is called a roux, pronounced *ROO*: equal parts fat and flour used to thicken sauces and gravies.) Stir in the stock and thyme, increase heat to medium-high, and bring to a boil. Reduce the heat to low. Season with bouillon, ½ teaspoon each of salt and pepper, and hot sauce and keep warm until ready to serve.

Serve the fried chicken with the gravy!

THE GRAVY

I've been frying chicken since I could spell "chicken." I find that the safest way of ensuring perfectly cooked fried chicken is finishing the bird in the oven. I'm aware that not everyone agrees with me, but especially if you're a novice fryer, having that perfectly golden crunchy outside means nothing if the chicken is raw on the inside. The catch-22 is to not overcook the bird in the oven. That's why using a digital meat thermometer is paramount (especially for newbies). I'm not sure which is worse, overcooked chicken or raw chicken; both are disgraceful, except that raw chicken is easier to recover. Anyway, I'll stop my rant. Happy frying :)

OVEN-FRIED STICKY GARLIC HENNY WINGS

SERVES 6 TO 8 **PREP TIME** 15 MINUTES **TOTAL TIME** 3 HOURS OR OVERNIGHT

2 pounds chicken wings, drumettes, and flats

2¼ teaspoons kosher salt

2 teaspoons baking powder

5 garlic cloves, grated

4 tablespoons (½ stick) unsalted butter

½ cup honey

1 cup Hennessy cognac

½ teaspoon crushed red pepper flakes

I should really call these my turn-up wings! It's boozed up and a dope party appetizer. I could tear up some wings, and by wings, I mean the whole wing: drumstick, flat, and the tips! Yes, please. I love that these wings are hella crispy, yet they are not deep-fried. These wings are bipartisan—everyone will love them, anyone can make them; even the chef will have an appetite to down them.

Place the chicken in a large bowl or airtight container and sprinkle with 2 teaspoons of the salt, the baking powder, and 1 teaspoon of the grated garlic. Mix together, cover, and refrigerate for at least 2 hours or up to overnight.

Set the oven racks in the middle and upper third of the oven. Preheat the oven to 450°F. Line a baking sheet with aluminum foil and set a wire rack on top.

Place the chicken on the prepared baking sheet. Bake on the middle rack until lightly browned on the first side, about 20 minutes. Flip the chicken, rotate the pan, and cook until very crisp and golden brown all over, 40 to 45 minutes more.

Meanwhile, in a saucepan, melt the butter over medium-high heat. Stir in the remaining garlic and cook until lightly golden, about 2 minutes. Remove the saucepan from the heat and add the honey, Hennessy, red pepper flakes, and remaining ¼ teaspoon salt. Return the skillet to medium heat. Cook, whisking occasionally, until the sauce is bubbling and thickened, about 5 minutes. Transfer the cooked wings to a large bowl and pour the sauce over the top. Toss well to coat.

Serve immediately.

SRIRACHA HONEY WINGS

SERVES 6 **PREP TIME** 5 MINUTES **TOTAL TIME** 25 MINUTES

Vegetable or peanut oil,
for frying

12 chicken wings
(about 3 pounds)

Kosher salt

½ teaspoon cayenne pepper,
plus a pinch

1 cup cornstarch

1 tablespoon smoked paprika

2 large egg whites

¾ cup Sriracha

¾ cup ketchup

⅓ cup honey

1 teaspoon grated fresh
ginger

2 teaspoons rice vinegar

1 teaspoon toasted
sesame oil

Black and white sesame
seeds, for serving

Chopped scallions,
for serving

These wings are tortorously good! I don't have a lot of favorite things like Oprah does, but the few favorite things I have, I cherish. Sriracha is one of my all-time favorite condiments. It should be its own food category . . . oh wait, it is. Ever since my days in college, you will always find me with a bottle of Sriracha in my bag, swag! I first made these wings in my college days and have been hooked ever since. Forgive me, these wings are like crack to my soul.

Fill a large skillet with vegetable or peanut oil to a depth of 2 inches and heat over medium-high heat to 350°F.

Season the chicken with ¼ teaspoon salt and a pinch of cayenne.

In a large bowl, whisk together the cornstarch, paprika, 1 teaspoon salt, and remaining ½ teaspoon cayenne. Put the egg whites in a separate shallow bowl.

Dredge the chicken in the cornstarch mixture and shake off any excess. Dip the wings in the egg whites, letting any excess drip off, then dredge in the cornstarch mixture again and shake off any excess.

Working in batches, carefully place the chicken in the hot oil and fry, turning occasionally, until the skin is crisp, and the inside is cooked through, about 10 minutes total. Transfer the chicken to a paper towel–lined plate to drain.

In a medium bowl, mix together the Sriracha, ketchup, honey, ginger, vinegar, and sesame oil. Add the cooked chicken wings to the sauce and toss to coat evenly.

Serve the wings garnished with sesame seeds and scallions.

MAPLE BOURBON BUTTERMILK FRIED CHICKEN

SERVES 6 TO 8   **PREP TIME** 15 MINUTES   **TOTAL TIME** 4 HOURS 45 MINUTES

SEASONING BLEND

2 tablespoons hot smoked paprika

1 tablespoon kosher salt

2 teaspoons freshly ground black pepper

1 teaspoon mustard powder

1 teaspoon garlic powder

1 teaspoon onion powder

1 teaspoon celery salt

½ teaspoon cayenne pepper

CHICKEN

2 cups buttermilk

½ cup bourbon

⅓ cup your favorite hot sauce

¼ cup maple syrup

2 garlic cloves, roughly chopped

12 chicken pieces

Peanut oil, for frying

2 cups self-rising flour

SAUCE

½ cup maple syrup

¼ cup bourbon

½ teaspoon crushed red pepper flakes

¼ teaspoon kosher salt

More on fried chicken, my friends . . . There are many roads that lead to good fried chicken. Let me tell you. I like to brine my chicken pieces. Brining makes the chicken more tender and imparts flavor. I choose to brine in one of my favorite boozes: bourbon. You could even get away with skipping the brine, instead just rolling the chicken in a seasoned flour mixture, letting it sit for a minute, then frying it. But then why make this recipe? The sexiest part is mopping the maple bourbon glaze on the fried chicken . . . ooo, baby!

Make the seasoning blend: In a small bowl, mix together the paprika, salt, black pepper, mustard powder, garlic powder, onion powder, celery salt, and cayenne.

Make the chicken: In a large bowl, combine the buttermilk, bourbon, hot sauce, maple syrup, garlic, and 2 tablespoons of the seasoning blend. Add the chicken pieces and turn to thoroughly coat with the buttermilk mixture. Cover tightly with plastic wrap and refrigerate for at least 6 hours and up to 24 hours.

Remove the chicken from the refrigerator at least 30 minutes before frying.

Preheat the oven to 375°F.

Fill a 12-inch cast-iron skillet two-thirds of the way up with oil and heat the oil over medium heat to 360°F. Line a baking sheet with aluminum foil and set a wire rack on top.

In a shallow dish, mix together the flour and 1 tablespoon of the seasoning blend. Remove the chicken from the buttermilk mixture, letting any excess drip off. Dredge the chicken pieces in the flour mixture so all sides are fully coated and shake off any excess flour.

Working in batches, add the chicken to the hot oil and fry, turning occasionally, until golden brown all over, 10 to 12 minutes total. Transfer the chicken pieces to the prepared baking sheet to drain. Repeat to fry the remaining chicken, adjusting the temperature of the oil as needed. When all the chicken has been fried, transfer the baking sheet to the oven and bake until the chicken has an internal temperature of 165°F, about 17 to 20 minutes.

Meanwhile, make the sauce: In a small pot, combine the maple syrup, bourbon, and red pepper flakes. Bring to a boil and boil for 2 minutes. Remove the glaze from the heat.

Serve the chicken hot, drizzled with the maple bourbon glaze.

This would be dope with some Eggo waffles! Just sayin' . . .

JERK CHICKEN

WITH *Mango Chutney*

SERVES 6 TO 8 **PREP TIME** 15 MINUTES **TOTAL TIME** 26 HOURS

8 to 10 chicken pieces, skin-on

2 cups Wet Jerk Marinade (recipe follows)

Canola oil, for grilling

1 cup your favorite BBQ sauce

½ cup low-sodium chicken stock

Mango Chutney (recipe follows), for serving

Rice and Peas (page 167) or cooked coconut rice, for serving

In my neighborhood on Springfield Boulevard, there's a spot called St Best Jerk Spot that jerks and smokes all day. You can smell the jerk blocks away; it's wonderful. I tear up at the smell of jerk thinking about its spicy punch, and because the way I feel about jerk could actually make me cry. Jerk chicken can be as spicy or as mild as you'd like it to be. I serve this with mango chutney on the side *fa cool it down real nice* <fake Jamaican accent>.

Place the chicken pieces in a bowl and coat with 1½ cups of the marinade, turning the pieces to coat evenly. Cover the bowl with plastic wrap and refrigerate for at least 8 hours and up to 24 hours.

Remove the chicken from the refrigerator 30 minutes before cooking.

Heat a grill to medium-high and rub the grill grates with oil.

Grill the chicken, skin-side down, until the skin turns golden brown and no longer sticks to the grill, 10 to 12 minutes. Flip the chicken and reduce the heat to medium. Cover the grill and cook the chicken until dark brown, about 30 minutes more.

While chicken is cooking, prepare the jerk sauce: In a medium saucepan, combine the remaining ½ cup marinade, the BBQ sauce, and the stock and bring to a boil. Cook, stirring occasionally, for about 5 minutes. Reduce the heat to low and simmer sauce for another minute. Set aside.

RECIPE CONTINUES »

THE GRAVY

For extra smoke flavor, use wood chips (apple, hickory, or pecan). Soak them in cold water for about 6 hours, then place them in a smoke tray or wrapped in aluminum foil (poke some holes in the top of foil to release the smoke) and set the tray directly over the coals in your grill. Cook the bird over indirect heat with the grill covered for smoky flavor.

Throughout the cooking, brush the chicken with the jerk sauce on all sides until completely lathered. The chicken is done when an instant-read thermometer inserted into the thickest part of the meat, not touching the bone, registers 165°F or higher.

Serve the jerk chicken with my mango chutney and rice and peas.

MANGO CHUTNEY

YEILDS 2 CUPS
PREP TIME 10 MINUTES
TOTAL TIME 25 MINUTES

1 tablespoon canola oil

1 small red onion, finely chopped

1 large garlic clove, minced

2 teaspoons grated fresh ginger

1 very ripe red mango, peeled and chopped

½ cup light brown sugar

⅓ cup golden raisins

¼ cup dried cranberries

1 tablespoon Jamaican-style yellow curry powder

½ teaspoon crushed red pepper flakes

¼ cup apple cider vinegar

Zest and juice of 1 lime

Heat the oil in a medium saucepan over medium-high heat. Add the onion and cook, stirring occasionally, until softened, about 3 minutes. Add garlic and ginger and cook, stirring occasionally, until fragrant, 1 to 2 minutes. Add the mango, brown sugar, raisins, dried cranberries, curry powder, red pepper flakes, and vinegar. Bring the mixture to a boil and cook, stirring occasionally, for about 5 minutes. Reduce the heat to low and cook until the chutney has thickened, about 10 minutes more. Transfer the chutney to a bowl and stir in the lime zest and juice. Let cool before serving or storing. The chutney will keep in an airtight container in the refrigerator for up to 1 week.

WET JERK MARINADE

MAKES 3½ CUPS
PREP TIME 5 MINUTES
TOTAL TIME 10 MINUTES

2 cups chopped yellow onions

2 cups chopped scallions

2 Scotch bonnet or habanero peppers

1 cup fresh cilantro

¼ cup mango nectar (I like Goya brand)

2 tablespoons soy sauce

1 tablespoon apple cider vinegar

1 tablespoon dark brown sugar

1 teaspoon browning sauce (see page 18)

1 teaspoon kosher salt

1 teaspoon freshly ground black pepper

1 teaspoon fresh thyme leaves (from 2 or 3 sprigs)

In the bowl of a food processor, combine all the ingredients and pulse until almost smooth but still slightly chunky. Store in an airtight container in the refrigerator for up to 1 week. Marinate food with the wet rub overnight for best results.

COCA-COLA–CANNED BBQ CHICKEN

SERVES 4 **PREP TIME** 15 MINUTES **TOTAL TIME** 1 HOUR 15 MINUTES

One (6- to 8-pound) whole roasting chicken, giblets removed

One (12-ounce) can Coca-Cola (keep the soda in the can)

1 tablespoon Dijon mustard

1 tablespoon packed light brown sugar

1 tablespoon smoked paprika

1 tablespoon canola oil

2 teaspoons chili powder

1 teaspoon garlic powder

1 teaspoon kosher salt

½ teaspoon freshly ground black pepper

¼ teaspoon cayenne pepper

¼ cup ketchup

Cooking a bird sitting up on a can? Sounds crazy and brilliant. This bird is handsome and sexy at the same time—I feel like it belongs in a museum. The smell of this bird cooking will make your nosy neighbors poke their heads out into your backyard. Cooking birds whole might seem a little intimidating, but there is nothing to fear. This recipe just requires you to get a little up close and personal with your bird. Let it know who's boss. And be fearless.

Put the chicken in a large zip-top bag.

Pour half the Coca-Cola (6 ounces/¾ cup) into a medium bowl, leaving the rest in the can. Add the mustard, brown sugar, paprika, oil, chili powder, garlic powder, salt, black pepper, and cayenne and whisk to combine. Pour the marinade over the chicken and massage it into the meat and skin (inside and out). Seal the bag and refrigerate for 4 hours or up to overnight.

Heat a grill to medium (or to 350°F). If using a charcoal grill, prepare the grill for indirect cooking at medium heat. Place a dripping pan in the grill directly underneath where the chicken will be cooked. (If you don't have a grill, preheat the oven to 350°F.)

Remove the chicken from the marinade and reserve marinade in the refrigerator for later use.

RECIPE CONTINUES ⟫

THE GRAVY

If you don't have a thermometer, poke a hole into the chicken thigh. The juices should run clear (never red or white).

Take the partially filled can of Coca-Cola and insert it into the cavity of the chicken so the chicken stands up, legs down and wings up. Tuck the wings to the back to prevent burning. Set the chicken, still on the can, on the grill grates directly over the dripping pan. Cover the grill and cook the chicken until the skin is crisp and an instant-read thermometer inserted into the thickest part of the thigh (without touching bone) registers 165°F, about 1 hour 15 minutes. If you're baking the chicken in the oven, set the chicken sitting on the can on a roasting pan and bake on the lower-third oven rack for 1 hour 10 minutes to 1 hour 15 minutes.

Transfer the reserved marinade to a medium saucepan, stir in the ketchup, and set aside. Bring the marinade to a boil, then reduce the heat to a simmer and cook until the sauce has thickened slightly and resembles BBQ sauce, about 15 minutes. Turn off the heat and set aside until ready to serve.

Transfer the chicken to a cutting board and let rest for 15 minutes before carving. Carve and serve with the sauce.

MOM'S CURRY CHICKEN

WITH *Red Hot Pepper Sauce*

SERVES 6 TO 8 **PREP TIME** 15 MINUTES **TOTAL TIME** 1 HOUR 30 MINUTES, PLUS MARINATING

¼ cup Jamaican-style yellow curry powder

1 tablespoon seasoning salt, such as Lawry's Seasoning Salt

2 teaspoons ground cumin

1 teaspoon ground coriander

¼ teaspoon cinnamon

8 bone-in, skin-on chicken pieces, such as legs and thighs

2 tablespoons canola oil

1 medium yellow Spanish onion, roughly chopped

4 scallions, chopped

2 medium carrots, sliced

2 medium russet potatoes, cubed

4 garlic cloves, chopped

1 tablespoon grated fresh ginger

Leaves from 4 sprigs fresh thyme

Kosher salt and freshly ground black pepper

1 Scotch bonnet or habanero pepper

Ain't That Easy . . . Roti (page 174), for serving

Rice and Peas (page 167), for serving

Red Hot Pepper Sauce (recipe follows), for serving

My mom's curry is the best curry I've ever tasted. She puts so much love in the food. Her recipe is so simple: lots of curry powder, onion, chicken, water, and salt. Of course, I wanted to "chef" it up. The first time I made this recipe, I asked her to taste it and she said, "You better not call this *my* curry." She did not approve, LOL. Mom has standards, and fortunately, I eventually succeeded. Mom's curry chicken is one of the closest things to my heart and always cheers me up. We love curry, white rice, roti, and cucumber tomato salads together in my house.

In a small bowl, mix together the curry powder, seasoning salt, cumin, coriander, and cinnamon. Place the chicken pieces in a large bowl and season with half the curry mixture. Cover and refrigerate for at least 30 minutes or up to overnight.

Heat the oil in a large Dutch oven or heavy-bottomed pot over medium-high heat until hot, about 2 minutes. Add the remaining curry mixture to the pot and toast, stirring with a wooden spoon, until very golden, 2 to 3 minutes. Add the chicken pieces, onion, scallions, carrots, potatoes, garlic, ginger, thyme, 1 teaspoon salt, and ½ teaspoon black pepper and cook, stirring occasionally and scraping up the seasonings from the bottom of the pan with the spoon, until the chicken is lightly browned, about 10 minutes. Reduce the heat to medium-low, cover the pot with a tight-fitting lid, and cook for 30 minutes. Do not add water at this point no matter how tempting. Remove the lid, add the Scotch bonnet whole, and stir in ½ cup water to thin out the gravy. Reduce the heat to low and cook until the chicken is fully cooked through and tender, about 30 minutes more. Remove the Scotch bonnet before serving. Season with salt and black pepper to taste. If the curry is too thick, stir in another ½ cup water.

Serve the chicken with my roti, rice and peas, and hot pepper sauce.

RECIPE CONTINUES »»»

THE GRAVY

Use gloves throughout the entire process. Make sure not to bring the peppers into direct contact with your skin or face.

RED HOT PEPPER SAUCE

YIELDS 4 CUPS
PREP TIME: 10 MINUTES
TOTAL TIME: 20 MINUTES

2 ounces red hot peppers (such as Jamaican hot peppers or habaneros), stemmed

10 garlic cloves

2 large cucumbers, peeled

½ cup white vinegar

1 lime, sliced

1 cup mango nectar (I like Goya brand)

2 teaspoons kosher salt

In the bowl of a food processor or blender, combine the peppers, garlic, cucumbers, vinegar, lime, mango nectar, and salt and process until smooth. Store the hot pepper sauce in sterilized mason jars or other airtight containers for up to 6 months. Use and enjoy with caution!

WHEN WE FORGIVE, WE GET BACK THE POWER TO BE HAPPY. WHEN WE HOLD ON TO ANGER, BITTERNESS, AND UNFORGIVENESS, WE ROB OURSELVES OF ABUNDANCE LOVE, JOY, AND PEACE. FREE YOURSELF WITH FORGIVENESS.

—Lazarus Lynch

MEATS
IS POPPIN'

CURRY LAMB MEATBALLS IN COCONUT SAUCE

SERVES 4 **PREP TIME** 15 MINUTES **TOTAL TIME** 1 HOUR 10 MINUTES

MEATBALLS

2 teaspoons coconut oil or olive oil

1 small onion, finely diced (about 1 cup)

1 small jalapeño, seeded and finely chopped (you could use half of one if you don't want it too hot)

3 garlic cloves, minced

2 teaspoons grated fresh ginger

1 pound ground lamb

2 tablespoons Jamaican-style yellow curry powder

3 tablespoons chopped fresh cilantro

1 teaspoon chopped fresh thyme leaves, plus 2 sprigs

1 teaspoon sweet smoked Spanish paprika

½ teaspoon ground cumin

½ teaspoon ground coriander

Kosher salt and freshly ground black pepper

1 large egg, beaten

3 tablespoons unseasoned Italian breadcrumbs

Meatballs are the best balls! The smell I get while making these reminds me of the aromas I experience when walking by the Halal Guys food trucks on Fifty-Third Street and Sixth Avenue around 1 a.m. They stopped serving lamb over rice and my heart skipped a beat. Can someone please confirm? Anyhow, when spices hit the heat, they suddenly wake up and start socializing. These meatballs are insane as a sub inside some crusty bread with chopped tomato and cucumber, fresh cilantro, and a squeeze of lime. You can also serve over basmati rice or with my Ain't That Easy . . . Roti (page 174).

Make the meatballs: Preheat the oven to 400°F. Line a baking sheet with parchment paper.

Heat 2 teaspoons oil in a large skillet over medium heat. Stir in half the onion, half the jalapeño, half the garlic, and half the ginger and cook, stirring occasionally, until softened, about 1 minute. Transfer the mixture to a large bowl and let cool for about 5 minutes, then add the lamb, 1 tablespoon of the curry powder, 1 tablespoon cilantro, chopped thyme leaves, paprika, cumin, coriander, ½ teaspoon salt, and ½ teaspoon pepper. Add the egg and breadcrumbs. Mix well. Shape the lamb into 16 golf ball–size meatballs and arrange them on the prepared baking sheet 2 inches apart. Bake until the meatballs are brown all around, about 10 minutes. Remove from the oven and set aside.

RECIPE AND INGREDIENTS CONTINUE ≫

SAUCE

½ teaspoon cumin

½ teaspoon coriander

⅛ teaspoon ground cinnamon

One (13.5-ounce) can unsweetened full-fat coconut milk

¾ cup low-sodium chicken stock

½ teaspoon sugar

Heat 1 tablespoon oil in the same skillet over medium-high heat. Add the remaining onion, remaining jalapeño, garlic, and ginger and cook, stirring occasionally, until softened, about 2 minutes. Stir in the remaining 1 tablespoon curry powder, the cumin, the coriander, and the cinnamon. Cook until fragrant and very brown in color, about 2 minutes. Whisk in the coconut milk, stock, sugar, ¼ teaspoon salt, and ¼ teaspoon pepper and bring to a boil, making sure there are no lumps. Reduce the heat to medium-low, then add the thyme sprigs and meatballs. Simmer the meatballs in the sauce until the sauce thickens, about 3 minutes. Stir in the lime juice. Taste and adjust the seasonings. Serve with the remaining 2 tablespoons cilantro.

SEXY ROAST PORK SHOULDER WITH CRANMUSTARD SAUCE

SERVES 12 TO 16   **PREP TIME** 20 MINUTES   **TOTAL TIME** 12 HOURS

PORK SHOULDER

One (6- to 8-pound) bone-in, skin-on pork shoulder, rinsed and patted dry with paper towel

6 large garlic cloves, finely chopped

Two (1.41-ounce) packets Sazón Goya seasoning

2 teaspoons dried oregano

2 teaspoons kosher salt

1 teaspoon freshly ground black pepper

2 cups low-sodium chicken stock

CRANMUSTARD SAUCE

One (12-ounce) package fresh or frozen cranberries

1 cup sugar

½ cup whole-grain Dijon mustard

THE GRAVY

When the pan juices have cooled in the measuring cup, the fat will rise to the top (it will have a whitish color). Spoon off the fat from the top and store the leftover juices in a container in the refrigerator for future use. Use the juices to make a gravy.

My pork shoulder needs lots of TLC, which is why it's so sexy. I marinate it overnight, give it some alone time in the oven, then serve it with my glamorous cranmustard sauce. I know the total time reads 12 hours, but this shoulder deserves it. The pork comes out succulent and falling off the bone. The best part is the leftovers, which can stretch you at least five new meals.

Make the pork shoulder: Set the pork shoulder fat-side up in a deep roasting pan. Use the tip of a sharp knife to carefully score the pork all over on all sides. (This will allow the seasonings to penetrate to the meat while it roasts.) Rub the entire pork shoulder with the garlic, Sazón, oregano, and black pepper, getting the seasonings into the crevices. Set the pork shoulder fat-side up and refrigerate, uncovered, for at least 6 hours and up to overnight.

Remove the pork from the refrigerator 30 minutes before roasting.

Set a rack in the lower third of the oven. Preheat the oven to 300°F.

Add the stock to the roasting pan and cover the roasting pan with heavy-duty aluminum foil. Roast the pork for about 5 hours 30 minutes, until the meat is tender. Remove the pork from the oven and let rest, covered, for 20 minutes.

Make the cranmustard sauce: In a small saucepan, combine the cranberries and sugar. Cook over medium heat, stirring occasionally, until the sugar has dissolved and the cranberries burst, about 5 minutes. Remove from the heat and stir in the mustard. Transfer to a small serving dish.

Slice the pork shoulder and carefully transfer the meat to a serving platter, along with pan juices. Serve with the cranmustard sauce!

PICKLED GREEN BEANS
(page 78)

CRISPY ESCOVITCH
FISH *(page 231)*

DR PEPPER UP MY SESAME RIBS

SERVES 4 **PREP TIME** 30 MINUTES **TOTAL TIME** 6 HOURS

½ cup packed light brown sugar

2 tablespoons smoked paprika

1 tablespoon chipotle chile powder

2 tablespoons garlic powder

2 teaspoons ground allspice

2 tablespoons kosher salt

1 tablespoon freshly ground black pepper

One (12-ounce) bottle Dr Pepper (about 1½ cups)

1 rack baby back ribs

1 tablespoon toasted sesame oil

2 teaspoons grated fresh ginger

2 garlic cloves, smashed

1 cup ketchup

¼ cup apple cider vinegar

2 tablespoons yellow mustard

1 tablespoon Worcestershire sauce

1 tablespoon white sesame seeds, for serving

1 tablespoon black sesame seeds, for serving

1 small bunch scallions, green parts only, finely chopped, for serving

My brain cells explode like Chance the Rapper's on *10 Day* when I taste ribs. I definitely stole this recipe to Food Porn Land. Have you ever been to that place? The cops tried to chase me down but I got away (just kidding—there's no such place . . . well, there kinda is). These ribs could not be easier to glow up. I literally dump sauce on top, throw them in the oven, and let them go. You could use any dark soda you want, but Dr Pepper's prescription is tested and legal. Sesame oil is a rockstar weapon in my kitchen, and a little goes a long way. These ribs are good vibes.

Line a roasting pan with aluminum foil.

In a small bowl, combine ¼ cup of the brown sugar, the paprika, chipotle powder, garlic powder, allspice, salt, pepper, and ½ cup Dr Pepper. Place the ribs meat-side up in the roasting pan and pour the brown sugar mixture on top of the ribs. Coat the ribs evenly with the spice rub and wrap tightly in plastic wrap. Refrigerate for at least 2 hours or up to overnight.

Preheat the oven to 300°F.

Remove the marinated ribs from the fridge 30 minutes before roasting. Remove plastic wrap and cover tightly with foil. Transfer to the oven and cook for 1 hour 30 minutes.

Heat the sesame oil in a saucepot over medium heat. Add the ginger and garlic and cook, stirring occasionally, until fragrant, 2 minutes. Add the remaining 1 cup Dr Pepper, the ketchup, remaining ¼ cup brown sugar, the vinegar, mustard, and Worcestershire. Bring to a boil, then reduce the heat to low and cook until the sauce begins to thicken, about 20 minutes. Remove from the heat.

RECIPE CONTINUES »»

Remove the ribs from the oven and brush half the sauce over the top and bottom of the ribs. Turn oven up to 375°F. Place the ribs back in the oven, uncovered, and cook for an additional 30 minutes. Remove the ribs from the oven and coat with more glaze. Return to the oven and cook, uncovered, until tender, about 20 minutes more. Coat with the sauce on both sides and place under the broiler for 3 to 4 minutes on each side.

Garnish with the sesame seeds and scallion. Slice and serve.

WILD <u>AND</u> CRAZY SWINEAPPLE HAM

SERVES 12 TO 15 **PREP TIME** 15 MINUTES **TOTAL TIME** 3 HOURS

One (6- to 8-pound) smoked ham

2 cups pineapple juice

½ cup Dijon mustard

½ cup packed dark brown sugar

1 tablespoon chopped fresh thyme

2 pounds smoked bacon (20 strips)

1 whole pineapple, peeled, cored, and sliced into fun shapes (rounds, squares)

1 cup fresh cherries, pitted

15 to 20 whole cloves

15 to 20 toothpicks or long bamboo skewers

This ham is a showstopper! It's wild! And it's definitely crazy! 'Nuff said.

Preheat the oven to 375°F. Set an oven rack in the middle position. Line a roasting pan with two sheets of aluminum foil and set a roasting rack in the pan.

Place the ham cut-side down on the roasting rack.

In a bowl, mix together the pineapple juice, mustard, brown sugar, and thyme. Set aside.

Place a large sheet of parchment paper on a flat surface. Arrange 10 slices of the bacon horizontally on the parchment, with ½ inch between each piece. Place 10 more slices of bacon vertically across the other pieces, weaving them together in an over-under pattern by lifting up alternating slices of the horizontal bacon and placing the vertical slices over or under them (think of a lattice design on top of an apple pie).

Lift the parchment paper and wrap the bacon around the ham, tucking the ends of the slices under the ham, if needed. Depending on the shape of the ham, sometimes it's easier to lay the ham on top of the bacon, then wrap the bacon around the ham. Decorate the ham with the pineapple slices, cherries, and cloves, holding the pineapple and cherries in place with toothpicks. Pour the pineapple juice mixture over the decorated ham. Roast until golden brown, about 2 hours 30 minutes (15 to 20 minutes per pound), basting every 30 minutes with the juices in the bottom of the roasting pan. Cover the ham with aluminum foil if the pineapples begin to brown too fast.

Carefully transfer the ham to a cutting board. Place the roasting pan on the stove and bring the liquid in the pan to a boil. Cook until the sauce thickens, about 12 minutes.

Serve the ham whole with the sauce poured over the top. Remove the toothpicks before slicing.

SMOTHERED PORK CHOPS IN COUNTRY GRAVY

SERVES 4 **PREP TIME** 15 MINUTES **TOTAL TIME** 1 HOUR

¾ cup all-purpose flour

1 tablespoon seasoned salt (such as Lawry's)

2 teaspoons roughly chopped fresh thyme, plus a couple of sprigs

2 teaspoons garlic powder

Freshly ground black pepper

2 tablespoons canola oil

2 tablespoons unsalted butter

Four (½- to ¾-inch-thick) bone-in pork chops

1 small bell pepper (whatever color you've got), sliced (about 1 cup)

1 small yellow onion, sliced

Kosher salt

2 cups low-sodium chicken stock

¼ cup heavy cream

I feel like a real southern boy when I eat smothered pork chops. My dad made fried pork chops every now and then, and would cover them in cream of mushroom sauce. These are fried until golden, then smothered in gravy. Everything is right about this dish.

In a shallow dish, mix together the flour, seasoned salt, thyme, garlic powder, and ¼ teaspoon black pepper. Spoon 2 tablespoons of the flour mixture into a separate small bowl and set aside.

Heat the oil in a large cast-iron skillet over medium-high heat.

Dredge the pork chops in the flour mixture and shake off any excess. Fry in the skillet until golden brown on both sides, 4 to 6 minutes per side, depending on thickness. Transfer the pork chops to a plate and cover loosely with aluminum foil to keep warm.

Reduce the heat to medium. Wipe out any remaining oil in the skillet with a paper towel. Add the butter, bell pepper, and onion to the skillet and cook, stirring often, until the vegetables are tender and softened, about 5 minutes. Season with ½ teaspoon salt and ¼ teaspoon black pepper. Add the reserved 2 tablespoons flour mixture and whisk until it forms a paste. Cook until the mixture is a deep golden brown, about 5 minutes. Add the stock and bring to a boil, stirring continuously to break up any lumps. Reduce the heat to medium-low and stir in the cream. Cook, stirring occasionally, until the sauce is thickened, 2 to 3 minutes. Taste and season with salt and black pepper.

Serve the pork chops on a platter or on individual plates with the sauce poured over the top.

PROSCIUTTO-WRAPPED TURKEY MEATLOAF

SERVES 6 **PREP TIME** 30 MINUTES **TOTAL TIME** 1 HOUR 30 MINUTES

KETCHUP GLAZE

½ cup ketchup

2 tablespoons Sriracha

1 tablespoon packed light brown sugar

2 teaspoons apple cider vinegar

MEATLOAF

1 tablespoon olive oil

1 small red bell pepper, finely diced (about 1 cup)

1 small yellow bell pepper, finely diced (about 1 cup)

½ yellow onion, chopped (about 1 cup)

2 garlic cloves, minced

2 pounds 80% lean ground turkey

2 sleeves Ritz crackers, crushed

2 large eggs, beaten

¼ cup buttermilk

1 tablespoon Worcestershire sauce

Pinch crushed red pepper flakes

Kosher salt and freshly ground black pepper

10 to 12 thin slices prosciutto (about 3 ounces)

What is it about a slab of meatloaf with mashed potatoes that feels so high school cafeteria to me? This low-key, low-class dish from the '50s still gets praise in my household. I've revamped it by wrapping the meatloaf in prosciutto (Italian dry-cured ham). You could be fancy and top your meatloaf with tomato sauce and basil you picked out of your garden, or keep it classic (like me) with a doctored-up ketchup. Welcome to my world.

Make the ketchup glaze: Using a small brush, in a small bowl, stir together the ketchup, Sriracha, brown sugar, and vinegar. Set aside.

Make the meatloaf: Preheat the oven to 350°F. Line a baking sheet with parchment paper or aluminum foil.

Heat the oil in a large skillet over medium-high heat. Add the bell peppers and cook, stirring occasionally, until softened, about 5 minutes. Add the onion and garlic and cook, stirring, until softened, about 3 minutes more. Remove from the heat and let cool.

Place the ground turkey in a large bowl. Add the crushed crackers, eggs, buttermilk, Worcestershire, red pepper flakes, 1½ teaspoons salt, and ½ teaspoon black pepper and mix to combine. Add the cooled vegetable mixture and mix well.

Transfer the meat to the prepared baking sheet and form it into a 10- to 12-inch oval. Brush the top and sides of the meatloaf with half the ketchup glaze. Wrap with the prosciutto, overlapping each slice slightly.

Bake until the prosciutto is crisp and golden, and the internal temperature is 160°F when inserted with a digital meat thermometer, about 1 hour. Brush the top and sides of the meatloaf with the remaining glaze and bake for 10 minutes more. Let the meatloaf rest for at least 10 minutes. Slice and serve.

FOOD TASTES THE BEST WHEN GRATITUDE IS THE FIRST BITE.

—Lazarus Lynch

see.food

BATTLE OF THE SEAFOOD

HABANERO BBQ SHRIMP SKEWERS

SERVES 4 **PREP TIME** 10 MINUTES **TOTAL TIME** 30 MINUTES

1 cup apricot preserves

Juice of 2 limes, plus wedges for serving

1 habanero pepper, seeded and small diced

2 tablespoons soy sauce

2 small garlic cloves, finely grated

1 teaspoon grated fresh ginger

2 pounds extra-large shrimp, peeled and deveined

Vegetable oil, for brushing

One Christmas, my brother, Joshua, gifted me a jar of Blue Diamond Habanero BBQ–flavored almonds. I OD'd on them. I think I almost licked the inside of the jar after eating all the almonds. I'm pretty sure I did. Yes, I know, I'm a weirdo, but so what. They were a mood! The flavor lingered in my mind and I thought it would be perfect for a grilled shrimp recipe. I love grilling shrimp, especially in the summer, because they take no time. Thanks to Blue Diamond and my brother for inspiring this recipe.

In a small bowl, mix together the apricot preserves, lime juice, habanero, soy sauce, garlic, and ginger. Transfer half the sauce to a large zip-top bag and add the shrimp. Seal the bag and refrigerate for 10 minutes.

Heat a grill to high or heat a large grill pan over high heat. Brush the grates or the pan with oil. Soak bamboo skewers in water and a wedge lime.

Thread 5 shrimp onto a bamboo or metal skewer (discard the sauce in the bag) and grill until charred on both sides, 4 to 5 minutes. Do not overcook, please.

Serve with the remaining sauce on the side for dipping and lime wedges.

THE GRAVY

Shrimp take no time to cook. Most people overcook them and they become tough and chewy. Also, wear gloves to protect your skin from the heat of the habaneros.

CURRIED SHRIMP <u>AND</u> OKRA

SERVES 4 TO 6 **PREP TIME** 15 MINUTES **TOTAL TIME** 45 MINUTES

2 tablespoons olive oil

½ yellow onion, chopped
(about ½ cup)

1 garlic clove, finely chopped

2 teaspoons grated fresh
ginger

1 tablespoon Jamaican-style
curry powder

1 teaspoon sugar

¼ teaspoon ground cumin

¼ teaspoon ground
coriander

One 14-ounce can stewed
tomatoes

One (13.5-ounce) can
unsweetened full-fat
coconut milk

1 cup low-sodium chicken
stock, plus more as needed

1½ teaspoons fish sauce

1 Scotch bonnet pepper,
or ¼ teaspoon cayenne
pepper (optional)

1 sprig fresh thyme

1 pound large shrimp,
peeled and deveined

½ pound fresh or frozen
okra, chopped into
½-inch-thick rounds

Kosher salt and freshly
ground black pepper

¼ cup fresh cilantro,
for serving

If, at this point, you haven't noticed my affinity for curry, then I just don't know what to say. We "curry" everything in my household. Curried chicken, curried goat, curried okra and shrimp. The list goes on and on. This is the seafood chapter, but the okra is really the star of this dish. Okra is exotic, and I don't find its texture to be a problem in this recipe, or ever, for that matter. This is a fast dish that's dope over white basmati rice.

Heat the oil in a deep skillet or heavy-bottomed pot over medium-high heat. Add the onions and cook, stirring often, until softened, about 2 minutes. Add the garlic and ginger and cook (but do not brown) until fragrant, about 1 minute. Add the curry powder, sugar, cumin, and coriander and cook for another minute. Stir in the tomatoes, coconut milk, stock, fish sauce, Scotch bonnet, and thyme. Bring to a boil.

Carefully remove the Scotch bonnet so as not to bust it and reduce the heat to medium. Stir in the shrimp and okra and cook until the shrimp are pink and tender and the okra is hot, 10 to 15 minutes. Season with salt and black pepper to taste.

Garnish with the cilantro and serve.

BEER-BATTERED POPCORN CATFISH BITES WITH LEMON-PEPPER DIP

SERVES 2 TO 4   **PREP TIME** 15 MINUTES   **TOTAL TIME** 45 MINUTES

LEMON-PEPPER DIP

1 cup mayonnaise

Zest and juice of 1 lemon

2 teaspoons coarsely ground black pepper

¼ teaspoon coarse sea salt

CATFISH BITES

Canola oil, for frying

1¼ cups all-purpose flour

1 teaspoon garlic powder

1 teaspoon sweet paprika

1 teaspoon coarse sea salt, plus more as needed

1 teaspoon baking powder

½ teaspoon baking soda

½ teaspoon freshly ground black pepper

two (12-ounce) lager beers, plus more as needed

1 tablespoon white vinegar

1 lemon, halved

Two (2- to 3-ounce) catfish fillets, cut into 1-inch squares

Chopped fresh dill, for garnish

Lemon wedges, for serving

I was a big fish-sticks-and-nugget kid back in the day. Well, I still am. I like the theory of a nugget: big flavor in a small package. These catfish bites are light, crunchy, and meaty. I enjoy dipping them in a doctored-up lemon-pepper mayo with a side of bread and butter pickles. These bites could even be wrapped in small soft tortillas, with a crunchy slaw, or wrapped in lettuce leaves. Maybe for the next book.

Make the lemon-pepper dip: In a large bowl, whisk together the mayonnaise, lemon zest, lemon juice, pepper, and salt. Cover and refrigerate until ready to use.

Make the catfish bites: Fill a cast-iron skillet with oil to come two-thirds of the way up the sides of the pan and heat over medium-high heat to 375°F. Line a baking sheet with paper towels, place a wire rack on top, and set it nearby.

In a large bowl, whisk together 1 cup of the flour, the garlic powder, paprika, salt, baking powder, baking soda, and pepper. Whisk in the beer and vinegar until smooth. The batter should resemble a loose pancake batter.

Put the remaining ¼ cup flour in a small bowl. Squeeze the lemon over the catfish pieces. Coat the catfish pieces with the flour, shaking off any excess, then dip them in the batter, allowing the excess batter to drip back into the bowl.

Working in batches, add the catfish pieces to the hot oil and fry, turning occasionally, until crisp and golden brown, about 2 minutes per side. Drain the catfish pieces on the prepared baking sheet and sprinkle with salt while hot.

Serve the bites with the lemon-pepper dip, a sprinkle of dill, and some lemon wedges.

CRISPY ESCOVITCH FISH

SERVES 4 **PREP TIME** 15 MINUTES **TOTAL TIME** 1 HOUR

1 cup white vinegar

2 teaspoons sugar

1 teaspoon whole black peppercorns

¼ teaspoon ground allspice

1 large yellow onion, sliced

1 medium carrot, finely grated

1 green bell pepper, thinly sliced

1 red bell pepper, thinly sliced

2 garlic cloves, minced

1 teaspoon grated fresh ginger

1 teaspoon fresh thyme

Two (3- to 4-pound) whole head-on red snappers, scaled and cleaned

Juice of 1 lemon

½ cup canola oil (or more as needed)

2 tablespoons seafood seasoning, such as Old Bay

1 cup all-purpose flour

There are two kinds of people in the world: people who eat fish with the head on, and people who don't. When I went to China, I ordered a whole fish from a restaurant, head on and everything. My host was surprised because she thought Americans don't eat like that. Well, she was wrong about this guy. You could make this recipe with any other fish, but red snapper is traditional. When choosing fish, make sure the eyes are clear and the fish doesn't smell like it's rotting. Anyhoo, here's to Escovitch!

In a large saucepan, combine the vinegar, sugar, peppercorns, allspice, and 1 cup water and bring to a simmer over medium heat. Cook, stirring to dissolve the sugar, for about 10 minutes. Turn off the heat and let sit for 5 minutes. Strain the vinegar and discard the peppercorns.

Place the onion, carrot, bell peppers, garlic, ginger, and thyme in a large zip-top bag. Pour the vinegar over the vegetables and seal the bag tightly. Refrigerate for 30 minutes.

Preheat the oven to 375°F. Line a baking sheet with parchment paper. Squeeze lemon juice over the red snappers on all sides. Let sit for 10 minutes.

Fill a large skillet with ½ cup canola oil and heat over medium-high heat to 360°F.

Combine the flour and the seafood seasoning together on a large plate or in a baking dish. Dredge the fish in the flour on both sides and shake off any excess. Fry the fish, one at a time, until very crispy on one side, then flip and fry until very crispy and golden brown on the second side, 8 to 10 minutes total. Place the fish on the prepared baking sheet. Repeat with the second fish.

Drain the vegetables and toss them with 1 tablespoon oil in a bowl. Scatter them on top of the fish. Transfer the fish to the oven and bake for about 10 minutes, until the vegetables are tender. Serve the fish right away with the vegetables on top.

PAN-SEARED SALMON WITH WHISKEY-HONEY GLAZE

SERVES 4 **PREP TIME** 5 MINUTES **TOTAL TIME** 25 MINUTES

One (8- to 10-ounce) skin-on salmon fillet, cut into 4 equal pieces

Kosher salt and freshly ground black pepper

2 teaspoons canola oil

¼ cup whiskey

2 tablespoons honey

1 tablespoon soy sauce

1 tablespoon fresh lime juice

2 or 3 fresh thyme sprigs

We are huge salmon eaters in my home. I find that the quickest way to cook salmon is to season it, crisp the skin in a smoking-hot skillet, then finish it in the oven. People overcook salmon all the time. It doesn't take a lot of time to cook, so don't walk away and forget about it (more on this in The Gravy). I love this whiskey-honey glaze on salmon, but it also rightfully belongs on any other roasted or grilled piece of fish.

Season the salmon with salt and pepper.

Heat the oil in a large skillet over medium-high heat until smoking, 3 to 4 minutes. Add the salmon pieces, skin-side down, and reduce the heat to medium. Gently but firmly press down the salmon with a fish spatula to ensure the skin has full contact with the heat and skin doesn't curl. Cook the salmon until very crisp, 5 to 6 minutes on the skin side. Flip the salmon and cook for 3 minutes more, then transfer to a plate. Remove the skillet from the heat, carefully drain the fat, and wipe the skillet clean with a paper towel.

In a small bowl, whisk together the whiskey, honey, soy sauce, and lime juice.

Return the skillet to the stove and pour in the whiskey glaze. Bring the sauce to a steady boil over medium-high heat, about 3 minutes. Add the thyme and cook until the sauce thickens and coats the back of a spoon, about 1 minute more. For a looser sauce, stir in 1 tablespoon water before removing the sauce from the heat. Discard the thyme sprigs and pour the glaze over the salmon.

Serve right away.

THE GRAVY

In general, I cook salmon to an internal temperature of 120°F to 125°F for medium-rare, and 125°F to 135°F for medium. Anything higher than 140°F is a NO-NO! Cooking salmon with skin-on protects the flesh of the salmon, reducing the likelihood of it drying out.

STEAMED CRAB LEGS

SERVES 4 **PREP TIME** 10 MINUTES **TOTAL TIME** 20 MINUTES

¼ cup seafood seasoning, such as Old Bay, plus more for serving

5 lemons: 3 sliced and 2 cut into wedges

12 crab legs

1 cup (2 sticks) unsalted butter

2 garlic cloves, minced

My family would take trips to the Chinese buffet back in the day and devour all of the crab legs. We would leave the restaurant smelling like a fish market. Dad steamed crab legs so much growing up and it was a huge family affair. I still love steaming up some crab legs and dipping them in hot, seasoned butter like Dad used to. I recommend serving this with my Jerk-Spiced Grilled Corn (page 146).

In a large pot over medium-high heat, bring 1 gallon water to a boil. Add the seafood seasoning and lemon slices, then reduce the heat to medium-low and simmer. Add the crab legs and cover the pot with a lid. Simmer until the crabmeat is cooked, 8 to 10 minutes. Remove from the heat and place the crab legs on a platter. Set aside.

In a medium saucepan, melt the butter with the garlic over medium heat, moving the pan in a circular motion occasionally.

Season the crab with additional seafood seasoning and serve with the melted butter and lemon wedges alongside.

CELEBRATE THE SMALL
VICTORIES. THE AIR
YOU ARE BREATHING,
THE HEART IN YOU
THAT IS PUMPING—
THESE ARE VICTORIES
ALL BY THEMSELVES.
CAN'T YOU SEE?

—*Lazarus Lynch*

GIMME SOME SUGA'

CLASSIC CARROT CAKE

SERVES 10 TO 12 **PREP TIME** 25 MINUTES **TOTAL TIME** 3 HOURS 55 MINUTES

CAKE

Unsalted butter, for greasing

2 cups sugar

1½ cups vegetable oil

4 large eggs

3 cups shredded carrots

2 cups all-purpose flour

1 cup chopped walnuts

½ cup golden raisins

1 tablespoon ground cinnamon

2 teaspoons grated fresh ginger

1 teaspoon baking powder

½ teaspoon ground nutmeg

½ teaspoon kosher salt

FROSTING

Two (8-ounce) packages cream cheese, at room temperature

½ cup (1 stick) unsalted butter, at room temperature

2 cups confectioners' sugar, sifted

1 teaspoon vanilla extract

1 cup chopped walnuts

I could go for a slice of this carrot cake every day for breakfast, lunch, and dinner. I would marry this cake. I would take naps with this cake. I would adopt this cake. Can you see I'm in love with this cake? You could easily eat a few slices and feel like you're flying. And no, the walnuts are not optional here!

Make the cake: Set a rack in the center of the oven. Preheat the oven to 350°F. Line two 9-inch round pans with parchment paper and grease with butter.

In a large bowl using a handheld mixer, beat together the sugar and oil on high speed until well combined. Add the eggs one at a time, beating after each addition, then beat the mixture until light and pale, about 5 minutes.

In a separate large bowl, combine the carrots, flour, walnuts, raisins, cinnamon, ginger, baking powder, nutmeg, and salt. Add to the bowl with the sugar mixture and beat on low speed until the flour is fully incorporated.

Divide the batter between the two prepared pans and place on the middle oven rack. Bake until the cakes are golden brown and a toothpick inserted into the center of each cake comes out clean, 45 to 48 minutes.

Run a knife around the sides of the cakes in each pan. Let cool completely in the pans on a wire rack for about 10 minutes, then flip the cakes onto the wire rack and remove the parchment paper. Let cool for at least 2 hours and up to overnight for best results.

Make the frosting: In a large bowl using a handheld mixer, beat the cream cheese on high speed until light and fluffy, about 3 minutes. Add the butter and beat until well combined and fluffy, about 2 minutes more. Shut off the mixer and add the confectioners' sugar and vanilla. Mix on low speed until well combined, about 1 minute. Chill the frosting for at least 15 minutes before using.

Assemble the cake: Place one cake layer, domed side-down, on a platter or cake stand. Fill the center with one-third of the frosting, leaving a ½-inch border. Place the second cake layer on top of the first, domed-side up. Working from the center, spread the remaining frosting over the top and up and down the sides of the cake to completely coat. Sprinkle with the chopped walnuts, slice, and serve.

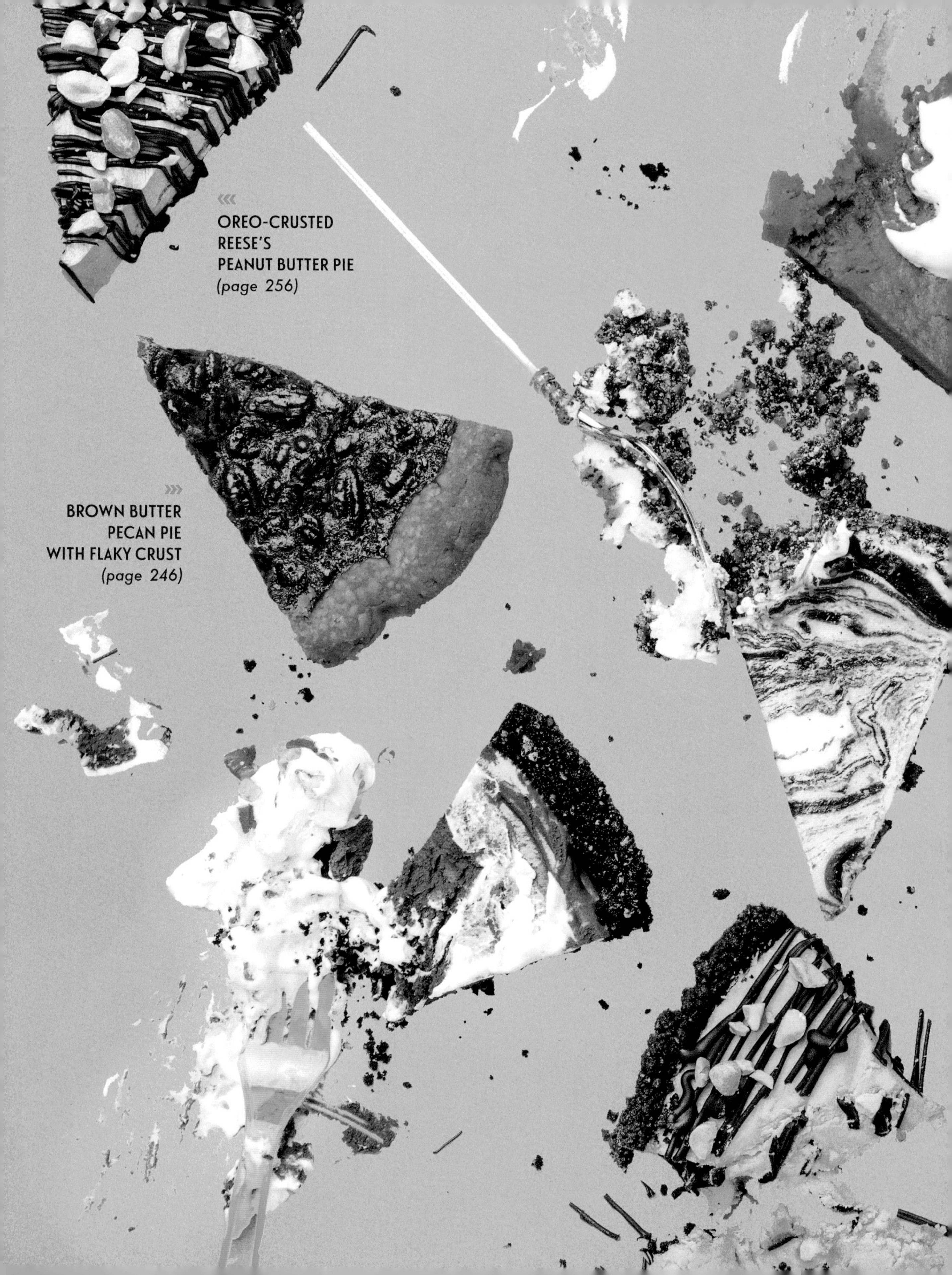

OREO-CRUSTED
REESE'S
PEANUT BUTTER PIE
(page 256)

BROWN BUTTER
PECAN PIE
WITH FLAKY CRUST
(page 246)

'BAMA MUD PIE MOUSSE
(page 254)

PUT THE
LIME IN THE COCONUT
RUM BARS
(page 250)

SWEET POTATO PIE
WITH GINGERSNAP-
PECAN CRUST
(page 252)

PRETZEL
CHOCOLATE
SWIRL CHEESECAKE
(page 248)

BROWN BUTTER PECAN PIE
WITH FLAKY CRUST

SERVES 8   **PREP TIME** 15 MINUTES   **TOTAL TIME** 2 HOURS 55 MINUTES

CRUST

1 cup all-purpose flour, plus more for dusting

2 teaspoons sugar

1 teaspoon kosher salt

½ cup (1 stick) unsalted butter, cut into cubes and chilled

¼ cup plus 2 tablespoons ice-cold water

1 tablespoon fresh lemon juice or apple cider vinegar

2 cups dried beans or pie weights, for baking

FILLING

5 tablespoons unsalted butter

3 large eggs

1 cup light corn syrup

⅔ cup packed light brown sugar

1 tablespoon vanilla extract

1 teaspoon fine sea salt

2 cups chopped pecans

Vanilla ice cream, for serving

My dad was known for his very sticky, ultra-sweet pecan pies. His mother could make a pecan pie better than anyone in the world, I'm told. I've upgraded this classic by using brown butter for a slightly nuttier appeal. I'm dreaming of a slice with some vanilla ice cream right now.

Make the crust: In the bowl of a food processor, combine the flour, sugar, and salt. Add the butter and pulse until the mixture has a coarse texture but the butter pieces are still visible, about ten pulses. Combine the ice water with the lemon juice in a measuring cup and slowly pour it in while pulsing the dough until it comes together, about ten more pulses. Turn out the dough onto a wide sheet of plastic wrap and flatten it into a 6-inch round. Refrigerate for at least 1 hour before using.

Remove the dough from the refrigerator and bring to room temperature, about 15 minutes.

Turn the dough out onto a lightly floured surface. Roll it into a 14-inch round and transfer to a 9-inch round pie dish, allowing the extra dough to hang over the edges. Press the dough into the bottom and up the sides of the pan. Trim the edges of the pie dough, leaving a 1-inch overhang. With floured fingers, fold the hanging dough over and crimp by pinching. Chill dough another 10 minutes in the freezer.

Place oven racks in the middle position. Preheat the oven to 425°F.

Remove the dough from the freezer and prick in several places (this will allow steam to escape and prevent the pie from bubbling up). Place the pie pan on a baking sheet. Line the dough with a large sheet of parchment paper. Pour dried beans or weights into the center of the parchment paper and flatten the beans into an even layer. Bake the crust until the edges are lightly golden, 12 to

15 minutes. Let cool before carefully removing the parchment and the beans (see The Gravy).

Reduce the oven temperature to 350°F.

Make the filling: Melt the butter in a small saucepan over medium heat. Allow the butter to bubble as the white foamy milk solids rise to the surface. Cook the butter, without stirring or moving the pan, until the milk solids become amber in color, about 4 minutes. Once the butter begins to brown and smell nutty, shut off the heat and immediately transfer the brown butter to a heatproof bowl and let cool.

In a large bowl, whisk together the eggs, corn syrup, brown sugar, vanilla, and salt. Fold in the pecans, then stir in the brown butter. Pour the mixture into the pie crust. Bake until the center is slightly jiggly and the crust is golden brown, 50 to 55 minutes.

Let the pie cool on a wire rack for at least 3 hours. Serve with vanilla ice cream!

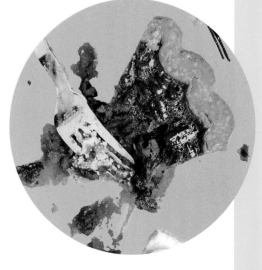

THE GRAVY

Blind baking is the process of lining pie crust with parchment and weighing it down with either dried beans, dried rice, or popcorn kernels to partially cook the dough before adding a filling. This ensures a thoroughly cooked crust. Nowadays, you can buy pie weights, designed for blind baking. I keep a small jar of dried beans exclusively for baking, and I use them again and again.

PRETZEL CHOCOLATE SWIRL CHEESECAKE

SERVES 10 TO 12 **PREP TIME** 15 MINUTES **TOTAL TIME** 9 HOURS

CRUST

1½ cups pretzel pieces

⅔ cup chocolate graham cracker crumbs (about 6 crackers)

¼ cup sugar

Pinch of fine sea salt

½ cup (1 stick) unsalted butter, melted and cooled

Cooking spray

FILLING

6 ounces semisweet chocolate morsels

Two (8-ounce) packages cream cheese, at room temperature

1 cup sour cream

3 large eggs

1¼ cups sugar

2 teaspoons vanilla extract

½ teaspoon kosher salt

Boiling water, for the pan

Desserts can be many things. I like the ones that talk sweet and talk salty like pretzels and chocolate. We need more of these happy things in the world! I will forever love making and eating this cheesecake. You too will be hooked once you taste this!

Make the crust: Preheat the oven to 325°F.

In the bowl of a food processor, combine the pretzels, graham crackers, sugar, salt, and pulse until coarsely ground, about 30 seconds. Add the melted butter and pulse until finely ground, five or six pulses.

Lightly coat the bottom and sides of a 9 x 3-inch springform pan with cooking spray. Line the bottom of the springform pan with aluminum foil. Press the crust into the bottom and up the sides of the pan.

Make the filling: Melt the chocolate morsels in a heatproof bowl in the microwave on high heat for 1 minute. Stir the chocolate until smooth, and cool completely.

In a large bowl using a handheld mixer or in the bowl of a stand mixer fitted with the paddle attachment, beat the cream cheese on low speed, scraping the bowl occasionally, until smooth, about 2 minutes. Add the sour cream and beat until creamy, about 1 minute. Add the eggs, one at a time, and beat until well incorporated. Add in the sugar, vanilla, and salt and beat on low speed until smooth. Pour the filling into the prepared pan. Drizzle the melted chocolate over the filling. Using a toothpick or bamboo skewer, swirl the chocolate with the filling (do not overmix—you want to keep the swirls distinct).

Place the springform pan in a large roasting pan and place them in the oven. Carefully fill the roasting pan with boiling water to come about halfway up the sides of the springform pan. (Be careful not to splash the cake with the hot water.) Bake for 1 hour 30 minutes, or until the cheesecake is lightly browned on top and the edges are set. Remove the pan from the water and let the cheesecake cool for 1 hour at room temperature. Loosely cover the surface of the cheesecake with plastic wrap and refrigerate for at least 6 hours or up to overnight to chill completely.

Remove the foil from the springform pan and run a knife along the sides of the cake. Release the springform from the cheesecake, slice, and serve.

PUT THE LIME IN THE COCONUT RUM BARS

SERVES 10 **PREP TIME** 10 MINUTES **TOTAL TIME** 3 HOURS 10 MINUTES

CRUST

Cooking spray

1 sleeve plain graham crackers (9 sheets)

¼ cup sweetened coconut flakes

1 tablespoon light brown sugar

4 tablespoons (½ stick) unsalted butter, melted

¼ teaspoon ground cinnamon

Pinch fine sea salt

FILLING

4 large egg yolks

Zest and juice of 4 limes

One (14-ounce) can sweetened condensed milk

1 tablespoon rum

¼ teaspoon vanilla extract

¼ cup sweetened coconut flakes

Okay, everyone, I have a little theory: If Kermit the Frog made these bars for Miss Piggy, they'd still be together. You guys remember the scene from *The Muppet Show* when Kermit severely twisted his flipper and the doctor gave him this weird and magical concoction: *"You put the lime in the coconut drink 'em bot' up."* If you don't know what I'm talking about, go and YouTube it right now, it's hilarious! Moral of the story: There is healing in these lime and coconut bars. For the record, most key lime bars suck (no shade), but the coconut and rum in these transforms them into a tropical, creamy, refreshing bite of sunshine (I'm clearly obsessed)!

Make the crust: Preheat the oven to 325°F. Spray the bottom and sides of a 9 x 11-inch baking pan with cooking spray. Line a baking sheet with parchment paper

In the bowl of a food processor, pulse the graham crackers, coconut, and brown sugar into a fine, sand-like texture. Add the melted butter, cinnamon, and salt and pulse until it comes together. Press the mixture evenly into the bottom of the prepared baking pan. Bake until lightly golden brown and set, about 10 minutes.

Make the filling: In a large bowl using a handheld mixer, whisk together the egg yolks, lime zest, lime juice, condensed milk, rum, and vanilla on medium-high speed until well combined and thickened, about 3 minutes. Stir in the coconut flakes until well combined. Pour the filling into the crust and bake until the edges are set but the center is slightly moving, 20 minutes. Cool for at least 30 minutes then refrigerate, uncovered, for at least 2 hours.

COCONUT WHIPPED TOPPING

1 cup heavy cream, chilled

¼ cup unsweetened coconut cream

2 tablespoons confectioners' sugar, sifted

¼ cup sweetened coconut flakes

Make the coconut whipped topping: In a chilled medium bowl using a handheld mixer, beat the heavy cream and coconut cream until it holds soft peaks. Add the confectioners' sugar on high speed until it holds soft peaks, about 5 minutes.

In a dry skillet over medium-high heat, toast the coconut flakes, moving them in the skillet occasionally, until light golden brown. Top the pie with the whipped topping and the toasted coconut flakes. Slice and serve.

SWEET POTATO PIE
WITH GINGERSNAP-PECAN CRUST

SERVES 8 TO 12 **PREP TIME** 20 MINUTES **TOTAL TIME** 6 HOURS 20 MINUTES

4 large orange sweet potatoes, rinsed

2 cups gingersnap cookie crumbs (about 36 cookies)

½ cup plus 2 tablespoons granulated sugar

½ cup pecans (optional)

¾ teaspoon ground cinnamon

½ cup plus 6 tablespoons (1¾ sticks) unsalted butter, melted and cooled

½ cup packed light brown sugar

2 large eggs, at room temperature

¼ cup heavy cream

1 tablespoon vanilla extract

½ teaspoon freshly grated ginger

⅛ teaspoon ground nutmeg

¼ fine sea salt

TOPPING

1 cup heavy cream

¼ cup confectioners' sugar, sifted

2 tablespoons maple syrup

Have you ever tasted Patti LaBelle's sweet potato pie . . . haha?! I must say, for a store bought pie, it is legit! Her biggest fan, James Wright, made a video about it on YouTube that went viral (it's worth watching). You can make this pie without the nuts and still be an awesome human! James, if you taste this pie, I welcome your review LMBO!

Line the middle oven rack with a sheet of aluminum foil. Preheat the oven to 400°F.

Using a fork, poke several holes in each potato, being careful not to poke yourself. Place the potatoes on a sheet of aluminum foil and place it straight onto the middle rack in your oven. Roast the potatoes for 1 hour to 1 hour 30 minutes, until tender. Remove the potatoes from the oven and let them cool down until you're able to handle them. Reduce the oven temperature to 375°F. Using a knife, slit a line down the center of the potatoes and peel off the skin using your hands. I personally like snacking on the skins, with olive oil and spices. Set the potatoes aside.

In the bowl of a food processor, pulse the gingersnap crumbs, 2 tablespoons of the granulated sugar, the pecans (if using), and ¼ teaspoon of the cinnamon to combine. Add 6 tablespoons of the melted butter and pulse again until combined. Pat the mixture into the bottom of a 9 x 13-inch baking dish and bake the crust until set, 12 to 15 minutes. Reduce the oven temperature to 350°F.

In the bowl of a food processor, combine the sweet potatoes, remaining ½ cup melted butter, the brown sugar, and the remaining ½ cup granulated sugar and process until smooth, scraping the sides down occasionally with a rubber spatula. Add the eggs, cream, vanilla, remaining ½ teaspoon cinnamon, the ginger, nutmeg, and salt, and blend until well combined. Scrape down the side of the bowl as needed to combine. Blend until thick and smooth, about 2 minutes.

Pour the batter into the crust and smooth out the top with a spatula.

Bake on the bottom rack of the oven until the center is set and the pie is firm, about 1 hour 10 minutes. Let cool completely on a wire rack for 3 to 4 hours.

Make the topping: In a large bowl using a handheld mixer or in the bowl of a stand mixer fitted with the whisk attachment, beat the heavy cream, confectioners' sugar, and maple syrup, until it holds peaks.

Slice the pie and serve with a dollop of the whipped topping.

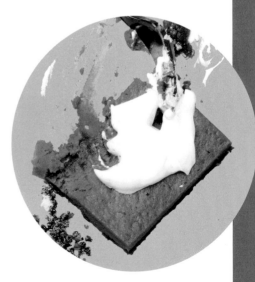

THE GRAVY

This might seem obvious, but when I say "sweet potatoes," I'm, talking about the long oval, brownish-skinned, orange-flesh sweet potatoes; not yams.

'BAMA MUD PIE MOUSSE

SERVES 8 **PREP TIME** 20 MINUTES **TOTAL TIME** 4 HOURS 45 MINUTES

CRUST

30 chocolate wafer cookies

⅓ cup chopped pecans

4 tablespoons (½ stick) unsalted butter, melted and cooled

CHOCOLATE MOUSSE FILLING

12 ounces bittersweet or semisweet chocolate chips

3 tablespoons unsalted butter

2 large pasturized egg yolks

1¼ cups heavy cream

2 tablespoons sugar

1 tablespoon instant espresso or coffee powder

1 teaspoon vanilla extract

TOPPING

1 cup heavy cream

3 tablespoons confectioners' sugar

1 tablespoon vanilla extract

½ cup pecans, roughly chopped, for serving

½ cup toffee pieces, roughly chopped, for serving

This pie reminds me of one of my favorite movie scenes from *The Help* when Miss Minny made a "chocolate pie" for Hilly. Hilly gagged and so did all of us watching! This scene has gone down as one of my most favorite-ever movie scenes. This ain't that kinda pie (let's just be clear LOL). Real talk: When Dad was a kid living in Alabama, he and his younger brother, Ronald, would make dirt pies literally from good ol' 'Bama dirt. Dad told me this story many times, so it inspired the creation of this recipe. I cannot get enough of this pie. I first debuted this recipe on Food Network's *The Kitchen*. It was a hit!

Make the crust: Preheat the oven to 350°F.

In the bowl of a food processor, pulse the cookies and pecans until finely ground. Add the melted butter and pulse until well combined. Press the mixture into the bottom and up the sides of a 9-inch deep-dish pie plate and bake until set, about 10 minutes. Place the pie plate on a rack to cool.

Make the chocolate mousse filling: In a medium microwave-safe bowl, combine the chocolate and butter and microwave for 30 seconds, then stir and microwave for 20 seconds more, until the chocolate has thoroughly melted and the mixture is smooth. Let cool. Whisk in the egg yolks, one at a time, and set aside.

In a medium bowl using a handheld mixer, beat the cream on medium speed until it holds soft peaks, about 4 minutes. Add the sugar, espresso powder, and vanilla and beat on high speed until it holds stiff peaks, about 3 minutes more.

Fold one-third of the cream mixture into the chocolate mixture and mix thoroughly until smooth. Transfer the chocolate to the bowl with the remaining whipped cream and gently fold it in until smooth and incorporated. Pour the filling into the prepared crust and chill for at least 4 hours before topping.

Make the topping: In a medium bowl using a handheld mixer, beat the cream on medium speed until it holds soft peaks. Add the confectioners' sugar and vanilla and beat at high speed until it holds stiff peaks.

Top the pie with the whipped topping, pecans, and toffee pieces. Serve.

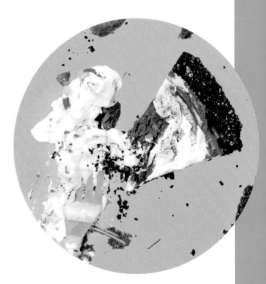

THE GRAVY

According to Wikipedia, pasteurized eggs are eggs that have been pasteurized. Make sense? I know. Not very helpful, LOL. Basically, pasteurizing eggs is the process of heat-treating the eggs before packaging to remove any harmful bacteria, making the eggs safe to eat raw or partially cooked. If you cannot find pasteurized shelled eggs, use pasture-raised eggs or 2 tablespoons liquid pasteurized eggs.

OREO-CRUSTED REESE'S PEANUT BUTTER PIE

SERVES 8 TO 10   **PREP TIME** 10 MINUTES   **TOTAL TIME** 4 HOURS

CRUST

8 ounces chocolate sandwich cookies, such as Oreos (about 20 cookies)

4 tablespoons (½ stick) unsalted butter, melted and cooled

Pinch of kosher salt

FILLING

1 cup heavy cream

1 cup plus 2 tablespoons smooth peanut butter

One (8-ounce) package cream cheese, at room temperature

1 cup confectioners' sugar, sifted

6 ounces dark chocolate chips

¼ cup chopped peanuts (optional)

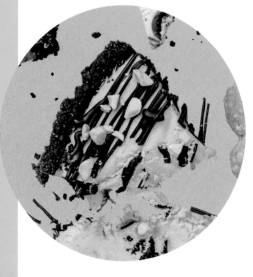

Living my best life over here with this pie! I devour peanut butter out of the jar for a living, and binge on Oreos while watching Netflix. I'm not surprised I created a recipe that couples two of my favorite food groups. As with all my other desserts, this one's here to slay.

Make the crust: Preheat the oven to 350°F.

In the bowl of a food processor, pulse together the Oreos, melted butter, and salt to form crumbs. Press the crumbs over the bottom and up the sides of a 9-inch pie dish. Bake until the crust is set, about 7 minutes.

Meanwhile, make the filling: In a large bowl using a handheld mixer, whip the cream on high speed until it holds firm peaks, about 3 minutes. Set aside.

In a separate bowl, mix 1 cup of the peanut butter, the cream cheese, and confectioners' sugar until smooth. Fold in the whipped cream and stir until smooth. Pour the peanut butter mixture into the prepared crust, smooth the top with an offset spatula, and refrigerate, uncovered, while you prepare the topping.

Place the chocolate chips and remaining 2 tablespoons peanut butter in a microwave-safe bowl. Microwave in 30-second intervals, stopping to stir between each, until melted and smooth, 60 to 90 seconds total.

Remove the pie from the refrigerator. Pour the chocolate mixture over the peanut butter filling in a zigzag motion in many directions to form your own unique design on top. Sprinkle the peanuts over the top of the pie. Refrigerate, uncovered, until set, about 3 hours, or freeze for 1 hour.

MOTHER SO-AND-SO'S LEMON POUND CAKE

SERVES 10 TO 12 **PREP TIME** 10 MINUTES **TOTAL TIME** 2 HOURS

CAKE

1 cup (2 sticks) unsalted butter, at room temperature, plus more for greasing

3 cups all-purpose flour, plus more for dusting

1 teaspoon fine sea salt

½ teaspoon baking powder

1 cup vegetable shortening

2½ cups sugar

5 large eggs

1 tablespoon vanilla extract

½ cup heavy cream

2 teaspoons grated lemon zest

¼ cup fresh lemon juice

ICING

2 cups confectioners' sugar, sifted

4 to 5 tablespoons fresh lemon juice

I grew up in a black Pentecostal church where Sunday services ended with a slice of cake. Mother Watkins was known for her lemon cakes and Mother Cherry for her lemon butter bars. We would tear it up! I never knew my paternal grandmother, but if she made lemon cake, I imagine it tasted like this.

Make the cake: Preheat the oven to 325°F. Grease a Bundt pan with butter and lightly flour it, tapping out any excess.

Sift together the flour, salt, and baking powder into a large bowl. Set aside.

In the bowl of a stand mixer fitted with the paddle attachment, cream together 1 cup butter, shortening, and sugar on medium speed until light and fluffy, about 5 minutes. Add the eggs, one egg at a time, beating after each addition, then add the vanilla. Scrape down the bowl with a rubber spatula. With the mixer on low speed, add half the flour mixture and half the cream and mix until the flour disappears. Add the remaining flour, remaining cream, the lemon zest, and the lemon juice. Mix just until the flour disappears. Using a rubber spatula, stir by hand to make sure everything is well combined.

Pour the batter into the prepared pan and bake until the cake has risen, the top is golden brown, and a toothpick inserted into the cake comes out clean, about 1 hour 10 minutes.

Let the cake cool in the pan on a wire rack for 30 minutes. Invert the cake onto a plate and let cool completely.

Make the icing: In a medium bowl, mix together confectioners' sugar and lemon juice until the sugar has completely dissolved. Pour the icing over the cake and serve.

DRUNKEN CHERRY DOUBLE CHOCOLATE ALMOND BROWNIES

SERVES 12 TO 16 **PREP TIME** 1 HOUR 20 MINUTES **TOTAL TIME** 2 HOURS 5 MINUTES

BROWNIES

1¼ cups fresh cherries, pitted

1 cup UV Cherry vodka

¾ cup all-purpose flour, plus more for dusting

1 cup (2 sticks) unsalted butter, cut into cubes and chilled, plus more for greasing

12 ounces semisweet chocolate chips

3 ounces unsweetened chocolate, roughly chopped

3 large eggs, at room temperature

1½ cups sugar

1 teaspoon vanilla extract

1 teaspoon almond extract

½ teaspoon kosher salt

1 cup slivered almonds

GANACHE

8 ounces dark chocolate

1 cup heavy cream

1 tablespoon unsalted butter, at room temperature

ASSEMBLY

⅓ cup slivered almonds, for serving

This recipe is nuts! The first time I made these brownies, I gave it a gold star. This recipe is blinging with gold stars. A good brownie has a nice crusty, crunchy top and an almost super-gooey center and is worth licking the excess chocolate off your fingers, very politely. What I really adore about these brownies are the drunken cherries, which I soak in cherry vodka overnight. I mean, seriously. These brownies are all that and a bag of *chocolate chips*. (See what I did there?)

Make the brownies: In an airtight container, combine the cherries and vodka. Cover and let stand at room temperature for at least 1 hour and up to overnight. (Do overnight. It's worth it.)

Preheat the oven to 350°F. Grease a 9 x 13-inch baking dish and line it with parchment paper, leaving a 1-inch overhang on two sides. Dust the dish with some flour, tapping out any excess.

In a microwave-safe medium bowl, combine the 1 cup butter, 8 ounces of the semisweet chips, and the unsweetened chocolate and microwave in 30-second intervals, stirring between each, until melted and smooth, about 2 minutes. Let cool.

In a separate bowl, mix together the eggs, sugar, vanilla, and almond extract (do not beat). Pour the cooled chocolate mixture into the egg mixture to combine.

Sift the flour and salt together into a medium bowl. Fold the flour into the chocolate mixture until the flour disappears. Do not over-mix. Fold in the remaining 4 ounces semisweet chips.

RECIPE CONTINUES »»

Drain the cherries, reserving the vodka. Fold 1 cup of the cherries and the slivered almonds into the batter. Set the remaining cherries aside.

Pour the batter into the prepared baking dish and bake until a toothpick inserted into the center comes out clean, 50 to 55 minutes. Transfer the pan to a wire rack to cool completely. Run a knife around the edges and lift the brownies out of the pan using the parchment.

Make the ganache: Place the dark chocolate in a medium heatproof bowl. In a small saucepan, bring the cream to a boil (the cream should almost boil over the pan). Immediately remove the saucepan from the heat and pour the hot cream over the chocolate chips and let it stand for 1 minute. Working from the center out, whisk the cream into the chocolate as it melts, until well combined and smooth. Add the butter and 2 teaspoons of the reserved cherry vodka and stir until the butter has melted and the mixture is well combined. Let cool for 15 minutes.

Assemble the brownies: Pour the ganache over the cooled brownies, using a spatula to evenly spread it over the top. Sprinkle with almonds and remaining ¼ cup cherries. Slice and serve.

THE GRAVY

Use leftover vodka for drinks.

DULCE DE LECHE BANANA PUDDING

SERVES 10 TO 12 **PREP TIME** 5 MINUTES **TOTAL TIME** 8 HOURS 5 MINUTES

1½ cups half-and-half

One (3.4-ounce) packet instant French vanilla pudding mix

One (8-ounce) package cream cheese, at room temperature

One (13.4-ounce) jar dulce de leche

1 cup heavy cream

¼ cup confectioners' sugar, sifted

One (7.25-ounce) package shortbread cookies, such as Pepperidge Farm

3 ripe medium bananas, thinly sliced crosswise (about 1½ cups)

Here's the thing: this banana pudding is actually life-changing. I've tasted every kind of banana pudding under the sun and here's my conclusion: very few are good. Banana pudding is a dessert that you either really love or strongly abhor. I get it, some people don't like the texture or smell of bananas (my mom is one of them). Others altogether hate pudding. Like, what did pudding ever do to anyone? But of course, who am I to try and convince you that your life will be significantly better when you eat this pudding, right? Whether it's all mental or something scientific going on with my taste buds, I can't stop eating this pudding. My brother makes an out-of-this-world stupid-good banana pudding that is just unnecessarily addictive, and it has inspired this one. It's just altogether borderline illegal. After making this, you might want to smack someone or get violent, so proceed cautiously.

In the bowl of a stand mixer fitted with the whisk attachment or in a large bowl using a handheld mixer, mix together the half-and-half and the pudding mix until well combined. Beat in the cream cheese and three-quarters of the dulce de leche. Stir until well combined.

In a separate large bowl using a handheld mixer, beat the heavy cream and confectioners' sugar on medium speed until it holds medium peaks, about 2 minutes. Fold the whipped cream into the pudding mixture by hand until well combined.

Arrange the shortbread cookies over the bottom of a 9-inch square dish. Spread a third of the pudding mixture on top of the cookies. Place a third of the banana slices on top and then spread a third of the remaining pudding mixture on top of the bananas. Repeat this process twice more with the remaining shortbread cookies, banana slices, and pudding mixture. Use a spatula to smooth out the top and sides. Cover with plastic wrap and refrigerate for 8 hours or up to overnight.

Warm the remaining dulce de leche in the microwave for 20 seconds, or until loose enough to drizzle.

Slice the pudding and serve with a drizzle of dulce de leche.

STICKY APPLE UPSIDE-DOWN BANANA CAKE

SERVES 8 TO 10   **PREP TIME** 20 MINUTES   **TOTAL TIME** 1 HOUR 20 MINUTES

TOPPING

½ cup (1 stick) unsalted butter, plus more for greasing

2 Golden Delicious apples, peeled, quartered, cored, and sliced ½ inch thick

1 cup packed light brown sugar

½ teaspoon ground cinnamon

Pinch fine sea salt

CAKE

⅔ cup packed light brown sugar

⅔ cup granulated sugar

2 large ripe bananas, mashed (about 1 cup)

½ cup unsweetened applesauce

⅓ cup canola oil

3 large eggs

2 teaspoons vanilla extract

2½ cups self-rising flour

1 teaspoon ground cinnamon

Pinch fine sea salt

¾ cup chopped pecans

I live for a rotting banana. The blacker, the better. I know once it turns brown, it gets really sweet and I can turn it into some confectionery delight. I wanted to create a cake that was banana bread meets pineapple upside-down cake meets hummingbird meets caramel sticky apples. I'm glad to say I've achieved that here. This cake is BOMBDIGGITY. BTW, I hope this picture turns you on. ❤

Preheat the oven to 350°F. Grease a 10-inch Bundt pan with butter, like a boss.

Arrange the apples in the bottom of the prepared pan and set aside.

In a medium saucepan, combine the butter, brown sugar, cinnamon, and salt. Cook over medium-high heat, stirring continuously, until you bring it to a bubble, about 3 minutes. Reduce the heat to medium-low and cook, stirring occasionally, until the sauce has thickened, about 2 minutes more. Pour the hot caramel mixture over the apples and along the sides of the pan (it's okay if the apples move while you're pouring in the sauce).

Make the cake: In a large bowl, mix together the brown sugar, granulated sugar, bananas, applesauce, oil, eggs, and vanilla. Mix in the flour, cinnamon, and a pinch of salt. Fold in the pecans with a rubber spatula. Pour the batter into the pan over the apples. Bake until the top is golden brown and a toothpick inserted into the cake comes out clean, 55 minutes to 1 hour.

Let the cake cool in the pan on a wire rack for just 5 minutes, then carefully and confidently invert it onto a plate. Do not be afraid. Let the cake cool completely before serving.

CHURROS WITH MEXICAN GANACHE

SERVES 12 TO 16   **PREP TIME** 15 MINUTES   **TOTAL TIME** 30 MINUTES

1¼ cups all-purpose flour

3 teaspoons ground cinnamon

½ teaspoon fine sea salt

1 cup whole milk

4 tablespoons (½ stick) unsalted butter

¾ cup sugar

2 large eggs

Vegetable oil, for frying

GANACHE

1⅔ cups unsweetened full-fat coconut milk

¼ teaspoon cayenne pepper

10 ounces Ibarra Genuine Mexican Chocolate (about 3 tablets), finely chopped or grated

At Roosevelt Avenue in New York City on the 7 train line, there's always someone selling fresh churros coated in cinnamon-sugary goodness. They cost like $2. It's the last place you'd expect to find churros, but they're pretty legit. Making churros at home is easier than you might imagine. First of all, it's FUN! I feel like a big kid at a carnival or the state fair. It's a lot like making funnel cakes. This very traditional Mexican dessert speaks to my very New York cultural upbringing.

Make the churros: In a medium bowl, combine the flour, 1 teaspoon of the cinnamon, and the salt.

In a medium saucepan, combine the milk, butter, and ¼ cup of the sugar and bring to a boil over medium heat, stirring until the butter has melted and the sugar has dissolved, about 5 minutes. Reduce the heat to medium-low. Add the flour mixture to the hot milk and stir vigorously with a wooden spoon until the mixture gathers into a glossy ball, about 1 minute. Remove from the heat.

Crack the eggs into a separate bowl. Beat one egg at a time into the warm saucepan until the dough has completely absorbed the egg. Mix until the dough is elastic and smooth. Let the dough cool completely.

Transfer the dough to a large piping bag fitted with a medium-size open star tip (a Wilton 1M or Ateco 847 tip will work).

In a wide dish, combine the remaining ½ cup sugar and 2 teaspoons cinnamon for coating the churros. Set aside.

Fill a wide pot with oil to a depth of about 2 inches and heat over medium-high heat to 350°F. Working in batches, pipe the batter into 3-inch segments straight into the hot oil, using a knife or scissors to cut off each segment before you pipe the next. Fry the churros, turning occasionally, until golden brown on all sides, 2 to 3 minutes per batch. Transfer the churros from the oil to a baking sheet lined with paper towel. Repeat to fry the remaining batter.

Make the ganache: In a saucepot, combine the coconut milk and cayenne and bring to a boil over medium-high heat. Place the chocolate in a large bowl and pour over the hot milk. Let sit for 1 minute, then stir until smooth and glossy. Let the ganache cool slightly before serving with the churros.

Roll the warm churros in the cinnamon sugar mixture to coat and serve with the ganache.

EDIBLE CHOCOLATE CHIP COOKIE DOUGH

MAKES 4 CUPS, TO SERVE 8 **PREP TIME** 10 MINUTES **TOTAL TIME** 35 MINUTES

1 cup (2 sticks) unsalted butter, at room temperature

1½ cups light brown sugar

2 tablespoons granulated sugar

2¼ cups all-purpose Page House Heat-Treated flour or gluten-free flour, if desired

¼ cup whole milk

2 teaspoons vanilla extract

1 teaspoon fine sea salt

1 cup chocolate chips (I personally like dark chocolate morsels, but semisweet work too)

Who else stuffs their face with cookie dough? I do! This dessert is every kid's dream come true. For those still in denial, you can come out from under your beds. This dough is addicting AF. You really shouldn't make this at home all by yourself, though. This is something to be shared scoop by scoop with all your friends. This recipe makes a ton of cookie dough, but I thought you guys would appreciate that. And you're welcome!

In a large bowl using a handheld mixer, cream together the butter and sugars until smooth, about 3 minutes. Scrape down the side of the bowl with a rubber spatula. Add the flour, milk, vanilla, and salt and beat until smooth. Fold in the chocolate chips by hand. Serve right away. Store, covered, in the refrigerator for up to 2 days.

THE GRAVY

I use Page House Heat-Treated flour for this recipe to ensure the raw dough is safe to eat. Trace amounts of harmful bacteria can be found in raw flour so heat-treated flour is great for uncooked, ready-to-eat recipes. I say, be safe.

To heat-treat flour at home, spread all-purpose flour on a baking sheet lined with parchment paper. Bake flour at 300°F for 15 minutes. Let cool before using. One cup of heat-treated flour is the same as 1 cup of all-purpose flour.

To turn the dough into cookies, preheat the oven to 350°F. Line a baking sheet with parchment paper. Add 2 large eggs, at room temperature, and ½ teaspoon baking soda to the dough and stir to combine. Scoop heaping tablespoons of the dough onto the prepared baking sheet leaving 1 inch between cookies. Bake until just golden around the edges, 10 to 12 minutes. Let cool on the baking sheet for 10 minutes.

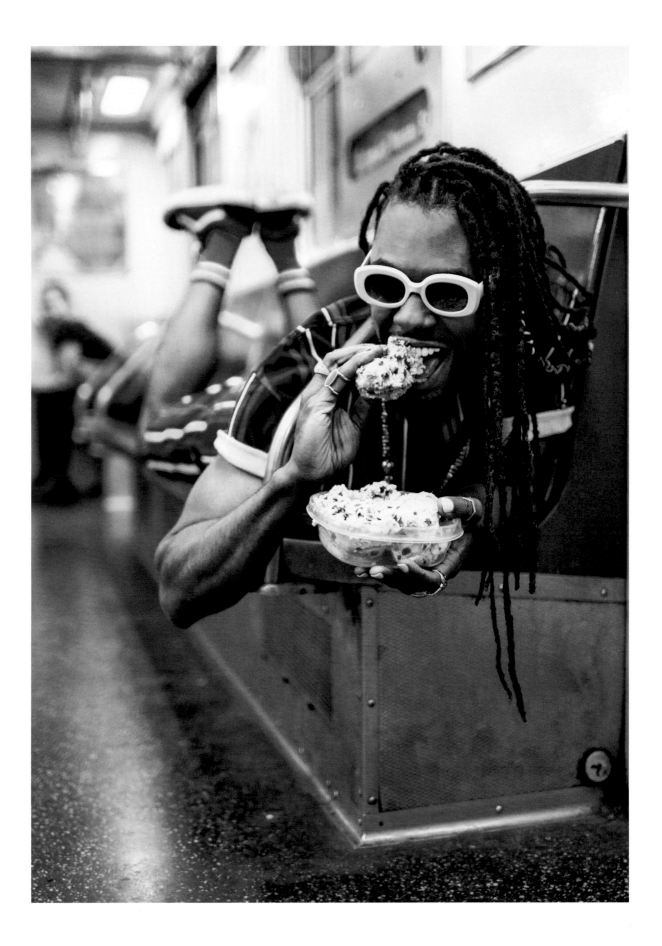

DOUBLE CHOCOLATE STRAWBERRY ICE CREAM SAMMICHES

SERVES 8 **PREP TIME** 15 MINUTES **TOTAL TIME** 45 MINUTES

Cooking spray

1 cup all-purpose flour

⅓ cup unsweetened cocoa powder

¼ teaspoon baking soda

¼ teaspoon fine sea salt

½ cup (1 stick) unsalted butter, at room temperature

¾ cup sugar

1 large egg, at room temperature

1 teaspoon vanilla extract

½ cup semisweet chocolate chips

½ cup white chocolate chips

Your favorite strawberry ice cream, slightly softened for scoopability

We always had ice cream sandwiches in our freezer growing up. They were late-night treats. Dad loved his Klondikes and I loved my ice cream sandwiches. These cookies alone are crazy good. I don't discriminate between my white and brown chocolate chips; they make my cookies extra special. These sammiches remind me of my childhood go-to, late-night sweet treats with Dad.

Preheat the oven to 350°F. Line two baking sheets with parchment paper and spray with cooking spray.

In a medium bowl, sift together the flour, cocoa powder, baking soda, and salt. Set aside.

In a large bowl using a handheld mixer or in the bowl of a stand mixer fitted with the paddle attachment, beat the butter and sugar on medium speed until smooth, about 4 minutes. Add the egg and vanilla and beat until well combined. With the mixer on low speed, add the flour mixture and beat until well combined and the flour disappears, about 2 minutes. Using a rubber spatula, scrape down the sides of the bowl to incorporate all the ingredients. Fold in the semisweet and white chocolate chips by hand.

Using a size-40 ice cream scooper, scoop 8 even mounds of the dough onto each prepared baking sheet. Bake until the cookies just begin to set, about 12 minutes. Let cool on the baking sheets, then transfer to a wire rack to cool completely.

Put a scoop of strawberry ice cream between two cookies and sammich together!

THE GRAVY

Feel free to substitute with pistachio or mint chocolate chip for the strawberry ice cream! And slay!

RED VELVET BROWNIES

SERVES 12 TO 24 **PREP TIME** 15 MINUTES **TOTAL TIME** 1 HOUR 25 MINUTES

BROWNIES

Cooking spray

2 cups all-purpose flour

½ cup unsweetened cocoa powder

½ teaspoon fine sea salt

1 cup (2 sticks) unsalted butter, at room temperature

3 cups sugar

4 large eggs, at room temperature

2 teaspoons vanilla extract

2 teaspoons white vinegar

2 tablespoons red food coloring

FROSTING

Two (8-ounce) packages cream cheese, at room temperature

4 tablespoons (½ stick) unsalted butter, at room temperature

2 cups confectioners' sugar

1 teaspoon vanilla extract

Pinch fine sea salt

Why is red velvet so popular? I've got to be honest, I don't love red velvet or brownies, but I've got so many feels for these red velvet brownies. I first debuted this recipe on my YouTube Channel in 2015. It was kind of a "whoops" recipe. I wanted to make a red velvet cake, and they turned out sort of cakey with a crunchy topping and crispy edges. Instead of forcing them to be something they didn't want to be, I let them be and I've been making them ever since. I'm very proud of these brownies. They put all other brownies to shame. They have restored my faith in red velvet and brownies.

Make the brownies: Preheat the oven to 350°F. Grease a 9 x 13-inch baking pan with cooking spray and line it with parchment paper, leaving some parchment hanging over two sides of the pan.

Sift together the flour, cocoa powder, and salt into a medium bowl. Set aside.

In a large bowl using a handheld mixer or in the bowl of a stand mixer fitted with the paddle attachment, beat the butter and sugar on medium speed until light and fluffy, about 3 minutes. Beat in the eggs, one at a time, until combined. Fold the flour mixture into the butter mixture with a spatula, then beat on medium speed until smooth. Add the vanilla, vinegar, and food coloring and mix until well combined. Use a rubber spatula to mix the coloring throughout.

Pour the batter into the prepared baking pan and bake until a toothpick inserted into the center comes out *almost* clean, about 45 minutes. Transfer the pan to a wire rack to cool completely, about 40 minutes (cheat by putting them in the freezer on a sheet tray!). Lift the brownie block from the pan using the overhanging edges of the parchment as handles. It's okay if it begins to crack a little on top.

Make the frosting: In a large bowl using a handheld mixer or in the bowl of a stand mixer fitted with the whisk attachment, whip together the cream cheese and butter until smooth, scraping down the sides with a rubber spatula as needed. Mix in the confectioners' sugar, vanilla, and salt until light and fluffy. Spread the frosting evenly on top of the cooled brownie block and cut the block into squares. Sprinkle any fallen crumbs on top of the frosted brownies and serve.

SWEET POTATO PECAN CINNAMON ROLLS WITH BOURBON GLAZE

SERVES 9 **PREP TIME** 20 MINUTES **TOTAL TIME** 4 HOURS 45 MINUTES

ROLLS

4 tablespoons (½ stick) unsalted butter

⅔ cup whole milk, at room temperature

½ cup sweet potato puree

1 teaspoon grated orange zest

3 cups all-purpose flour, plus more as needed

One (¼-ounce) packet active dry yeast (2¼ teaspoons)

½ cup packed dark brown sugar

½ teaspoon ground cinnamon

½ teaspoon fine sea salt

1 large egg

Canola oil, for greasing

Dear Sweet Potato Pecan Cinnamon Rolls with Bourbon Glaze,

I dream of you when I wake

I want you more than cake

Your glistening charm runs down your sides

You're better than a piece of pie

I never knew a love like this

Live in all your sexy bliss!

P.S. Everyone deserves to experience these warm, sweet, boozy buns.

Make the rolls: Melt the butter in a small saucepan over medium heat. Remove from the heat and add the milk to warm. Transfer the milk mixture to the bowl of a stand mixer fitted with the paddle attachment and beat in the sweet potato puree and orange zest.

In a separate bowl using the handheld mixer, whisk together the flour, yeast, brown sugar, cinnamon, and salt. With the stand mixer on low speed, add the flour mixture and mix until combined. Beat in the egg, then beat until the dough comes together. Switch to a dough hook attachment and beat on medium speed until the dough forms a ball. If dough is too sticky, add more flour 1 tablespoon at a time.

Flour your hands and turn the dough out onto a floured surface. Knead the dough until smooth and elastic, about 5 minutes. Form into a ball. Transfer to a lightly oiled bowl. Cover the dough with plastic wrap or a dish towel and set aside at room temperature until doubled in volume, 2½ to 3 hours.

RECIPE AND INGREDIENTS CONTINUE ≫

FILLING

1 cup sweet potato puree

½ cup packed dark brown sugar

4 tablespoons (½ stick) unsalted butter, melted and cooled, plus more for greasing

1 tablespoon vanilla extract

1 teaspoon ground cinnamon

1 teaspoon ground ginger

½ teaspoon fine sea salt

½ cup chopped pecans (optional)

TOPPING

¾ cup packed dark brown sugar

2 tablespoons bourbon

1 cup confectioners' sugar

2 tablespoons unsalted butter

1 teaspoon vanilla extract

½ cup pecans, chopped, for serving (optional)

Meanwhile, make the filling: In a medium bowl using a handheld mixer, beat together the sweet potato puree, brown sugar, melted butter, vanilla, cinnamon, ginger, and salt.

Turn the dough out onto a floured work surface and roll it into a 9 x 13-inch rectangle. Spread the sweet potato filling in the center of the dough using an offset spatula, leaving a ½-inch border. Sprinkle the chopped pecans (if using) evenly over the filling.

Starting at one long side, tightly roll up the dough, jelly roll–style. Place the dough seam-side down and cut it crosswise into 9 equal pieces.

Grease a 9-inch cast-iron skillet with the remaining butter. Place the rolls in the skillet, cut-side up (to see the circular rings) and touching one another. Cover with plastic wrap and a dish towel and set aside at room temperature until doubled in volume, about 45 minutes.

Preheat the oven to 375°F.

Remove the dish towel and plastic wrap and bake the rolls until golden brown, about 30 minutes.

Make the topping: While the rolls bake, in a small saucepan, combine the brown sugar, bourbon, and ¼ cup cold water and cook over medium-high heat, stirring, to dissolve the sugar, about 5 minutes. Whisk in the confectioners' sugar, butter, and vanilla until a smooth and pourable glaze is formed, 1 to 2 minutes more.

Remove the cinnamon rolls from the oven and let cool slightly, 2 to 3 minutes. Pour the glaze on top of the rolls and sprinkle with the pecans (if using). Let the glaze set for about 20 minutes before serving.

RUM RAISIN PLANTAINS FOSTER WITH VANILLA ICE CREAM

SERVES 4   **PREP TIME** 10 MINUTES   **TOTAL TIME** 30 MINUTES

3 tablespoons unsalted butter

½ cup packed dark brown sugar

¼ teaspoon ground cinnamon

2 ripe sweet plantains, sliced on an angle into ½-inch-thick pieces

¼ cup raisins

¼ cup dark rum

Vanilla bean ice cream, for serving

Coarse sea salt, for serving

This is probably the easiest dessert in this book. Rum and raisins are a flavor match made in heaven. I love bananas Foster, and substituting for sweet plantains was a no-brainer. For this recipe, you want to wait until your yellow plantains are black, black, black. If you're not a baker, you will impress yourself with this dessert. The salt on top makes you want more.

Melt the butter in a large nonstick skillet over medium heat. Add the brown sugar and cinnamon and cook, stirring, until the sugar has dissolved, about 2 minutes. Add the plantains and move them around in the pan to evenly coat them with the butter and sugar. Add the raisins. Remove the skillet from the heat briefly and add in the rum. Return the pan to medium heat and cook until the alcohol has evaporated, 5 to 7 minutes. (The alcohol may catch on fire; don't fret! Just step back and let the fire cook out the alcohol.)

Scoop some vanilla ice cream into each of four bowls. Pour some plantains and sauce over the ice cream. Sprinkle with sea salt and serve.

THE GRAVY

Plantains are different from bananas; you cannot eat them raw. You can make plantains ripen faster by placing them into a paper bag on your kitchen countertop until they turn black.

SKILLET BERRY CRISP WITH ALMOND-CORNMEAL TOPPING

SERVES 8 TO 10 **PREP TIME** 10 MINUTES **TOTAL TIME** 1 HOUR

CRUMBLE TOPPING

½ cup all-purpose flour

⅓ cup sliced almonds

¼ cup yellow cornmeal

¼ cup lightly packed light brown sugar

Pinch fine sea salt

4 tablespoons (½ stick) unsalted butter, at room temperature

FILLING

2 pints fresh blueberries

Two (6-ounce) packages fresh raspberries

2 tablespoons cornstarch

½ cup packed light brown sugar

1 tablespoon fresh lemon juice

1 teaspoon ground cinnamon

Vanilla ice cream, for serving

Skillet fruit crisps are probably my number-one go-to for desserts because they're so easy to make. You just toss fruit with sugar and cornstarch, then top them with a mixture of butter, brown sugar, oats, and flour, and it's lit. I wanted to switch up the usual oats topping, so I chose a cornmeal-and-almond version, which, let me tell you, makes my oat version look sorry. I love this crisp warm out of the oven with a scoop of cold vanilla bean ice cream on top. I don't want to be bothered when I'm here. Don't call me. Don't text me. Please, just let me have my moment.

Make the crumble topping: Preheat the oven to 375°F.

In a large bowl, combine the flour, almonds, cornmeal, brown sugar, and salt. Add the butter and mix using your fingers until the mixture is crumbly. Refrigerate.

Make the filling: In a 10-inch cast-iron skillet, combine the blueberries, cornstarch, brown sugar, flour, lemon juice, and cinnamon. Mix together with a spoon. Remove from the fridge and evenly sprinkle the crumble mixture on top of the berries. Bake until the fruit mixture is bubbling and the top is golden brown, 30 to 35 minutes. Let cool.

Serve warm with a scoop of vanilla ice cream!

DAD'S PEACH COBBLER

SERVES 10 TO 12 **PREP TIME** 20 MINUTES
COOK TIME 50 MINUTES TO 1 HOUR **TOTAL TIME** 2 HOURS 45 MINUTES

CRUST

3 cup all-purpose flour, plus more for dusting

3 tablespoons sugar

2 teaspoons kosher salt

¾ cup (1½ sticks) unsalted butter, cut into cubes and chilled

1 cup ice-cold water, plus more as needed

FILLING

3½ pounds fresh peaches, pitted and quartered or two (29-ounce) cans peaches, drained

1 cup sugar

¼ cup all-purpose flour

1 tablespoon ground cinnamon

½ teaspoon freshly grated nutmeg

Fine sea salt

TO ASSEMBLE

1 large egg, beaten

Ground cinnamon, for dusting

Sugar, for dusting

Ice cream, for serving

What can I say? This is one recipe I will cherish for the rest of my life. It warms my heart when I think about how many times my dad made this cobbler, how many times he watched his mother make it, and how much it means to our family. This recipe will never get old.

Make the crust: In the bowl of a food processor, pulse together the flour, sugar, and 2 teaspoons salt until just combined. Add the butter and pulse a few more times until the mixture is coarse but the butter pieces are still visible. Slowly add the ice water and pulse to form a dough, six to eight pulses. If the dough looks and feels very dry, add more ice water, 1 tablespoon at a time. Divide the dough in half and wrap each half tightly in plastic wrap; flatten each piece into a disc. Refrigerate dough for 1 hour.

Make the filling: In a large bowl, mix together the peaches, sugar, flour, cinnamon, nutmeg, and a pinch of salt. Set aside.

Preheat the oven to 375°F.

Remove the dough from the refrigerator and cut in half. On a lightly floured surface, roll it into a 9 x 13-inch rectangle, about ¼ inch thick. Set aside and repeat with the second piece of dough.

Line a deep 9 x 13-inch baking dish with one of the dough rectangles, pressing any excess dough against the sides of the dish. Pour in the peach filling and spread it evenly. Place the second rectangle of dough on top of the peaches and tuck the excess dough into corners. Brush the dough with the beaten egg and sprinkle with cinnamon and sugar. Pierce the top with the tip of a sharp knife in several places to allow steam to escape while baking. Bake until the top crust is golden brown, about 1 hour 15 minutes. Let cool on a rack before serving. Serve with ice cream.

SON OF A SOUTHERN CHEF CREDITS

AVERY
an imprint of Penguin Random House
New York

VICE PRESIDENT AND PUBLISHER
Megan Newman

EXECUTIVE EDITOR
Lucia Watson

EDITORIAL ASSISTANT
Suzy Swartz

ASSOCIATE ART DIRECTOR
Ashley Tucker

MARKETING AND PUBLICITY DIRECTOR
Lindsay Gordon

PHOTOGRAPHY, PRODUCER, AND GRAPHIC DESIGNER
Anisha Sisodia

AGENT
Jane Dystel

RECIPE TESTERS
Ashley Diedrick and Claudia Sidoti

LEAD FOOD STYLIST
Graciel Caces

ASSISTANT FOOD STYLISTS
Anthony Michael Contrino,
Enrique Gatchalian (aka Pancho),
Dawn Miller, Jahqyad Austin, Miracle Lynch

CULINARY FLOATER
Sam Chang

FASHION STYLIST
Keeon Mullins and Windy Lawrence

PROPS STYLING
Lori Tannis

HAIR
Sabina Clarke, Denise Pinnock, Vickie Lee

MAKEUP
Miracle Lynch

NAIL TECHNICIAN
Rita Saha

SPECIAL THANKS TO
Mom, Dad, Little Ray (Shank), Joshua Lynch,
Lauren Lynch, Miracle Lynch, Sarah Jane
Coolahan, Scott Feldman, Ali Wald,
Georgia Tollin, Two Twelve Management,
Jaimie Roberts, Michael Hafitz, Jason Barth,
Debra Park, April Baptiste-Brown,
Susan Stockton, Ingrid Hoffmann,
Ellie Krieger, Denise and Lester Bourne,
Camilo Perdomo, Brandon Blackwood,
Vania and David Jewelry, Applejack Diner,
Brooklyn Diner, National 4-H Council,
Roger Turgeon and Food and
Finance High School,
the World Food Prize Foundation,
family, and friends

INDEX

Page numbers in *italics* refer to photos.